MIKE MURPHY

"I could write a book...so I did"

MIKE MURPHY

"I could write a book...so I did"

Inside Stories from My 46 Years in Radio!

With Steve Jackson

Foreword by Charles Gusewelle

KANSAS CITY STAR BOOKS

STAR
BOOKS

"I could write a book...so I did"

Inside Stories from My 46 Years in Radio!

by Mike Murphy with Steve Jackson

Copyright © 2008 by Mike Murphy

Edited by Donna Martin
Design by Vicky Frenkel

Published by Kansas City Star Books, An imprint of *The Kansas City Star*

To order copies, call StarInfo (916-234-4636 and say "Operator").
www.TheKansasCityStore.com

First edition, first printing
Printed in the United States of America by
Walsworth Publishing Co., Inc., Marceline, Missouri

ISBN 10: 1-933466-85-5
ISBN 13: 978-1-933466-85-9

Library of Congress Control Number: 2008931419

Kansas City Star Books
Kansas City, Missouri

STAR
BOOKS

This book is dedicated to the following people:

Cathy, my dear wife of forty-eight years, to my great kids, Pat, Susan, and Jenny, and to Cy Perkins, Pat O'Neill, Larry Stewart (Secret Santa), Walt Coffey, Carl J. DiCapo, FS Meatsauce (Greg Schmidt), Patricia Schmidt, Tom Leathers, and Dr. Rich Davis.

CONTENTS

FOREWORD

From the 1970s until 2004, Mike Murphy was the radio voice of Kansas City.

Athletes, politicians, tycoons, and notorious crooks come and go on the public stage. But celebrity is perishable. The collective memory is short.

There are, however, notable exceptions. And Mike is one of them.

For the guests who joined him on the air, some of them many times – luminaries as varied as Charlton Heston and Liberace, Omar Sharif and John McCain, Pearl Bailey and Barry Goldwater – the invitation to share a microphone with Murphy gave them welcome exposure to an important heartland audience.

And for his many thousand fans, his retirement meant a wrenching change in the pattern of their days. Because to them – listeners of all ages, ethnicities and occupations – the Mike Murphy call-in program was a regular, ongoing conversation with a man they knew and liked.

Thanks to this collection of rich memories and anecdotes, long-time admirers can experience that fun again. And those too young to have shared the Murphy addiction can find here a sampling of what they missed.

My own first time on the show was in 1980, and as a stranger to radio

I was nervous going in. He quickly put me at ease. His on-air manner – relaxed, playfully good-natured and thoroughly Irish – was immediately reassuring.

His nimble intellect let him engage with guests on subjects that ranged from sports to politics, from food and music to the Loch Ness monster and UFOs. And he never was impressed by his own importance. That came through to me as it did to his listeners, many of whom he knew by name and by the sound of their voices on the phone line.

Radio and newspapering are quite different vocations, but our careers have had some parallels. We've both spent a half-century at our crafts, and both been witness to watershed changes in the industries to which we've devoted our lives.

It was Mike, not long after that initial date on his show, who encouraged me to write a book. And I've been an enthusiastic cheerleader for the writing of his.

With his daily show, Mike Murphy set a high mark for the radio hosts after him to aim at. Apart from that, his contributions to the texture of life in our city have been many: the St. Patrick's Day Parade, the Cattle Drive through Downtown, his fund-raising activities on behalf of the Salvation Army, and other worthy causes.

His talent has earned him the admiration of his colleagues and many high professional honors.

But you can be sure no recognition has pleased him quite as much as knowing there's a multitude of good folks out there who, though they've never met him, call him their friend.

— C. W. Gusewelle

INTRODUCTION

As I'm sitting here doing this, with my brilliant, magical, mathematical brain, I just figured out it was fifty years ago – *fifty years ago!* – that I got into the radio business. It was June of 1958.

I started at KLEE Radio, "*1480 on your dial.*" They had me doing mornings, I'd oversleep, Cathy and Sister Louise and Mom… all those people would call me to get me up in the morning to turn the transmitter on.

I'd often blow out the transmitter bulbs, because they were supposed to warm up for an hour before you started broadcasting, but I'd just go down, turn 'em on and start broadcasting away. *And ba-looey!* There went the bulbs.

Anyway, I stayed at KLEE for a year and then went to Springfield, Illinois, and had a great time there. Actually I was there twice. But Springfield was a great town and I made some great friends. We even had a reunion a couple of years ago.

Those were great days in early radio. We played our own records, picked 'em all, the ones we wanted to play. I played Buddy Holly and the Crickets, the Big Bopper, Ritchie Valens… and I remember the day their plane went down in Clear Lake, Iowa. What a tragedy.

But I went on and did it for forty-six more years – till 2004. As I write this book, it's actually fifty years, and I'm still messing around doing commercials and newspaper ads.

In the sixties, we'd listen to disk jockeys all over the country and do what they did. There were some really good ones like Wally Phillips in Chicago on WGN and the McKinnon Brothers, Don and Doug, at KIOA in Des Moines. They called me one day and wanted me to come to KIOA, but at that time I was doing pretty well. Too bad, though, the McKinnon Brothers were the best I ever heard.

The business has changed so much. The disk jockeys today don't have much freedom to say what they want, and they can't become the local personalities like we used to.

After businesses deregulated, big corporations began buying up dozens, maybe hundreds, of local stations, and creating specific formats – Pop, R&B, Country, Oldies – and you were supposed to play what was on their play list.

Then the corporate people came up with this new thing called "voice tracking," and that's where one guy can go into the studio and record four hours' worth of sound bites in twenty minutes, intros to the records or the news and weather. It makes it sound like somebody is there but there isn't. It's real fabricated and impersonal.

Before that there were owners of stations that you knew. I worked for a guy named Bill O'Connor, and Frank Babcock, G. Laverne Flambo, Ken Spangler, and Al Evans. All these guys – the owners of the stations – became great friends.

But today they've been replaced by corporations. The deregulation allowed one corporation to buy up eight stations in a single market – a whole city, town, whatever. They'd buy up the top eight stations and the smaller guys wouldn't have a chance. They'd change the call letters. (The marketing people told them that high-scoring Scrabble letters – Z, Q, X, J, K – are more memorable, so when you see a station with those letters in their names, there's a good chance it's part of a corporate conglomerate.)

But to do what I did for forty-six years, through all the trends and all the changes… I don't know many people who've done it that long.

Especially in today's bottom line, "run it as cheap as you can" philosophy. That's really why I left. One of the corporations came in, fired a bunch of my friends and cut my pay in half.

And that was standard practice. Big corporation buys the station, sends in some young whiz kid who'd fire half of the people and cut the salaries of the others in half. I'm sure it looked great on the bottom line of some-body's spread sheet. But it sounded boring and redundant and uninspired. These are tough times in the radio business. My hat is off to anyone who can hack it.

But all in all, it was a good ride, a long ride, a fun ride. The wonderful, brilliant people I worked with and played with, the great friends I made along the way, the witty, nutty, crazy people that made my life so terrific, the people like John Wayne and Steve Allen and Barry Goldwater, who I got to talk to and sit down with.

I used to say to my good friend, Charles Gusewelle, "You know, Charles, what you do is on paper and a hundred years from now people will be able to go to a library or somewhere on the Internet and find what you've written and be moved by it. All of my words went into the air – as far as I know they're still going – but there's very little left of what I said." Maybe the aliens and space people heard me and made a record of it.

I used to think that twenty years from now, nobody will ever know that I existed. Through the years I had a lot of people come up to me and say, "Why don't you write a book?" And I'd say, "I don't have stories that people would want to hear." It just never entered my head as to how I'd actually do it. Then I met my friend, Steve Jackson, and he said, "Let's just sit down and you can tell me some stories. I'll have a digital recorder going and we'll see what happens." Well, this is what happened.

So to all those people out there who said I should write a book, well, I did! And maybe a hundred years from now somebody will pick up this thing you're holding, blow the dust off, read it, and think, "I'll be damned. That was a hell of a guy. Good thing he wrote a book."

Hope you like it,
— *Mike Murphy*

BISHOP FULTON J. SHEEN

The morning we left for Ireland, Cathy and I went to pick Dan Hogerty and his wife, Lillian, up at his house, and who was there to see us all off but our good buddy Jim Lynch to wish us all the luck of the Irish. What a great guy! So we get to Ireland in time to see the St. Patrick's Day festivities in Dublin. And one of those nights we were sitting in the dining room at the Gresham Hotel on O'Connell Street. Dan looked behind us back in the corner and he said, "Oh my God, do you know who that is back there?" I look around and say, "No, I don't." He said "It's Bishop Sheen!"

Bishop Fulton J. Sheen had become an American folk hero in the fifties and sixties. His prime-time television show, *Life Is Worth Living*, often challenged or beat out other legendary prime-time shows such as Milton Berle, Frank Sinatra, and Ed Sullivan. He was watched by millions. There was nothing like him and probably never will be again. What a passionate, charismatic, and witty soul.

So Dan said, "You know I actually met Bishop Sheen about twenty years ago when my son, Dennis, was at Notre Dame. I bet he'd remember me." And I said, "You know, Dan, I bet he would, too," although I was pretty sure he wouldn't. Well, in the meantime, I see Bishop Sheen get up and go to the men's room. So I excuse myself and follow him in there. So when I get in there, all of a sudden I'm taking a whiz right alongside Bishop Sheen. Now this is an event in itself. How many people can say they've taken a whiz alongside Bishop Sheen?

But I got my nerve up and said, "Bishop? I'm with a man named Dan Hogerty who says you'd remember him when you met him and his son, Dennis, twenty years ago at Notre Dame." And the bishop smiled and said, "Young man, tell me this story again."

The bishop was known for his great sense of humor. So I told him the story again. He said, "What's the man's name?" I said, "Dan Hogerty." "And his son's name?" I said, "Dennis." He said, "I've got it."

So we finished up and I went back to our table and after a couple of minutes pass, Bishop Sheen comes over, looks at Dan and says, "Dan Hogerty! I remember you. I met you twenty years ago at Notre Dame. Your son's name is Dennis, right?" Well, Dan looked up at me and he burst into tears. He said, "You see? I told you he'd remember me." It was amazing. We all want identity and want to be remembered. That's one of my favorite stories.

A LITTLE WEIRDNESS

This is just a little story. You know, I did so many shows about the paranormal and magic and flying saucers and ghosts... you know, weird stuff. Weirdness. I never really had that many paranormal experiences myself, but sometimes things happen that make you wonder. This is kind of one of those.

There was a priest I used to have on the show named Father Tom Cummings, who was president of Rockhurst High School, a great Jesuit and a great friend of mine. I used to have him on when anything about religion came up or needed talking about.

Well, Father Tom got transferred to Denver, but before he left, there was this fund-raiser sale they used to have at Rockhurst called "Sale-O-Rama." And right after this time he brought me a shirt from there that looked old and it had a picture on it of somebody fishing in the water somewhere, in a canoe. Really horrible looking. It was something you'd probably never wear. When I got home I threw it in the closet and forgot about it.

I think it was about ten years after that, and I hadn't seen Father Tom in all that time. But one night the doorbell rings and there he is, big as life. And he said, "Can I come in and spend the night?" And I said, "Sure."

So he comes in and sits down and says, "What is that shirt you have on?"
I looked down and said, "Father, that's the shirt you gave me ten years
ago from Sale-O-Rama. This is the first time I've had it on since you gave
it to me. I didn't know you were coming. I went to the closet this morning
and saw that shirt and for some reason I put it on."

Now, what the hell is that?

OTTUMWA

I was born in 1939 on July 15 at St. Joseph's Hospital in Ottumwa, Iowa. The first memory I have, when I was about three and a half, my mom, or somebody, came to me and said, "Your dad was killed yesterday." I was just a little kid and I remember telling my mom, I said, "Oh, Mom, he's not dead. He just burned his arm." But I remember that, and so Mom raised me and my brother and sister from the time I was three and a half and they were ten and eleven. Mom settled with the railroad… He was killed on the railroad one day in January. I've always hated January. It's a depressing time of the year. And I had a rich uncle, my uncle Bill, and he came to Mom and he said, "Let's just settle with the railroad on this." My mom had lawyers coming in from all over the country to sue the railroad and make a lot of money on this. But my uncle Bill came to Mom and said, "Why don't you just settle?" And the railroad's offer to my mom, to raise three kids, was $5,000!

Now five thousand bucks in those days was probably about a hundred thousand bucks today. So she got $5,000 to raise three kids, feed 'em, get 'em through school and college and everything. But we also got passes on the railroad for life! We probably used them ten times. It was a bad deal.

My poor mom had just been a housewife, so she went to work at Yonker's Department Store for forty years, standing on her feet, waiting on people, stocking clothes, trying to put together enough money to get us kids through school. There was my brother, Pat, who was handsome as a prince and smarter than a wizard and he was my hero. He could play basketball like nobody I ever saw, and shoot pool better than Minnesota Fats, but that story's somewhere else in the book.

Anyway, that's kinda the way I began in Ottumwa, Iowa. And from the time I was in first grade, I knew I had to get out of there.

Ottumwa was a depressed town. Most of the people were depressed because it was a few rich and a whole lot poor, not much in the middle. There was the North Side – the doctors, dentists, lawyers, bankers — and there was the South Side – railroad workers and factory workers and people that worked at the John Morrell meat packing plant.

Incidentally, that's where Tom Arnold worked when he was in high school. Tom Arnold was the most famous person ever to come out of Ottumwa, I guess. I was until he came along and married Roseanne. And my wife, Cathy, went to school with Tom's mother. Her name was Linda Arnold.

So I was a kid during the forties, and like I said, it was a tough time. We were all kinda the same – nobody had anything. At Christmas we'd get just one thing -- a sled, a toy, a new pair of shoes. I remember one time when I got a new pair of shoes. I slept with them on because I didn't want anyone to come in the house and steal them.

One time my mom lost her job and she had to move to Sigourney, Iowa, to work for the state government. And so my sister, Patricia, stayed to watch over me. And she wound up having seven kids -- six girls and a boy -- and her son, Greg, my nephew, is now my great friend, "FS Meatsauce," that I often talk about from time to time. I see him at least once every week. He's a great man.

Anyway, in the forties it was really tough back then in Ottumwa. The winters were cold and the snow was deep. My friend Birdhouse and I used

.

to talk about getting out of there one day. At our school, the nuns were just about what you hear they were like. You know those leather winter hats with the strap and the buckle? Well this one nun used to beat me across the face with it and I said to myself, "I'm never gonna let anyone hit me again." And I haven't.

In seventh grade, Sister Rosemary took a liking to me and would let me do anything. One time I'd shinnied up this pole in the middle of the room and I was hanging up there making faces and in walked the bishop. And there I was atop this pole and the bishop looked at Sister Rosemary and said, "What's he doing up there?"

She said, "I don't know how he got up there, Bishop." So I got on down, but I still remember she'd let me do anything. She was a great old gal and I loved her.

Eighth grade it was Sister Clementine, and Sister Clementine didn't know what anybody's name was. She was kind of out of it. She called us by where we sat in the class: "Boy in the back seat!" "Boy in the front seat." But eventually it ended up that we were the first class to graduate from this new St. Mary's School that I was the janitor of. I wasn't the janitor, but I was the assistant janitor to a guy named Leif Ladd, who told all of us all the dirty jokes he'd ever heard in his life.

"There was an old hermit named Dave…" "There once was a man from Nantucket…" and all those old things and I always remembered those dirty jokes and especially the limericks. They were the best. "When I was young and had no sense, I da-da-da-da on an electric fence…"

Then on to high school. And all this time I would walk to school from our apartment up on Market Street, down the hill and through the Ottumwa Hotel.

And when I'd get to the corner there, where I'd catch the bus, I'd go over to Walsh High School, which was named after Monsignor Walsh. It was an all boys' Catholic high school. Anyway, I'd be standing on the street and I'd think, "I wonder what's going to happen to me?"

And one day, twenty-five or thirty years later I guess it was, I came to the Ottumwa Hotel to stay for a reunion we were having and I was at the very same place. I was in the car and I turned on the radio and got KCMO down here and they were playing one of the *Best of Murphy* shows that were so popular. And so after all those years of wondering what was going to happen to me, there I was, sitting in my car in front of the Ottumwa Hotel, listening to myself interview Omar Sharif on the radio in Kansas City. And it was like I was in a time machine. I'd come full circle. I finally knew what was going to happen to me. It really blew my mind.

BOUNCING AROUND

Before I came to Kansas City in 1968, I'd been in the business for ten years and had a series of moves and jumps from town to town. I was working as a DJ playing records of all kinds. I started in Ottumwa, Iowa, then went to Springfield, Illinois, then Cedar Rapids, Iowa, then Peoria, Illinois, then back to Springfield, then to Moline, Illinois, where I became good friends with a man named G. Laverne Flambo. Then I went to Indianapolis and got fired there and went back to Moline. When we added it all up, we made thirteen moves in eleven years!

Finally I got an on-air audition in Philadelphia with their number one station, WIP. After the audition I went out to lunch with one of the station guys named Alan Hotland, I think, and he told me I'd come in second for the job. So I got the desire to work in a big town with a big market. Indianapolis had been great and I'd loved working there, but a lot of people said it was "asleep" and they called it "Nap Town." Since then I hear it's really come alive.

So when I got back to Moline from Philly, I was itching to get out of there to a big city as fast as I could. So the guy in Philadelphia remembered me and he recommended me to a guy in Kansas City. So that guy called and said, "Would you have any interest in coming to Kansas City?" And I said, "I wouldn't go to that town if you paid me $500,000 a year!" I'd remembered going through it when I was a kid and I just didn't like what it looked like. On the other hand, it wouldn't hurt to take another peek.

Lenny and Jim and Dan and Me

So as fate would have it, I got recommended for a job that was coming up at a station called KMBZ. And a guy named Walt Lochman, whom I have hundreds of stories about, called me and said to come on down. So I came down from Moline, where there was about three feet of snow on the ground, and got to Kansas City, where there was no snow and it was warm, and I thought, "Man, this is the tropics! Maybe this'd be all right!" So I auditioned and they hired me at union scale, which wasn't much, but it was more than I was making in Moline, and it got me away from all that snow up north.

When I came down to work at KMBZ, their program director, a guy named John Holliday, said, "Let me introduce you around to our news people and our sports people." Well, the news people were great and when we went over to meet the sports people. He said, "I want you to meet our sports director." And I said, "Who's that?" And he said, "Len Dawson." So we go into the sports room and there's Len sitting there in the flesh. He was wearing what looked like an $800 suit and he was as handsome as a movie star. I thought to myself, "Boy, this is the big time. I'm gonna be working with Len Dawson?" And then Len said, "Come down the hall and meet the guy who substitutes for me," and it's Chiefs' linebacker, Jim Lynch, who I'd been a fan of since his days as an All-American linebacker at Notre Dame. So there they were, these two football heroes, who would lead the Chiefs to their first Super Bowl in 1970. We would become great friends.

One day Jim Lynch said, "I want to take you down the street to meet a friend of mine named Dan Hogerty." This was the beginning of my great friendship and great times with Dan Hogerty and Len Dawson and Jim Lynch. And one day I said to Dan, "Dan, we're gonna go to Ireland."

By that time, I was really on a roll around here. I'd taken the station from a 7 rating to almost a 50, I had higher name recognition than the mayor, and the station would pretty much support anything I wanted to do. I could say I wanted to go to Mars or the Moon or go look for the Loch Ness Monster...and they said, "Yeah! That's a great idea. Look for the Loch Ness Monster." So I went to the station manager, Walt Lochman, and said, "I want to go look for the Loch Ness Monster!" And he said, "Whatever you say!" So Dan and I and our wives set off to search for Nessie. But before we got to Scotland, we stopped in Ireland for St. Patrick's Day.

ART BELL

One of the most fun guests I ever had on the show was Art Bell. He hosted the nationally syndicated show *Coast to Coast A.M.*, which at its peak had more than five hundred radio stations, and was supposed to have upwards of 30 million listeners.

One particular year - I think it was 1998 - I had the great fortune to win the Marconi Award, radio's highest honor, the Academy Award of Broadcasting. I didn't know I was gonna win it and the boss of the station said, "Don't bother to go to Seattle for the ceremony because you're not gonna win it." He wanted to go.

Well, I did win it and the program director, Bill White, got up and accepted it. I heard the tape of it. "Accepting the award for Mr. Murphy..." blah, blah, and they had the orchestra playing. It was truly a great honor.

So that was '98. And the Art Bell people got wind of that. I'd had Art on my show as a guest. Art was taking some time off and they called and said, "Would you do the weekends?" I said I would. And I did and what a kick it was. Broadcasting to 20 or 30 million people a night. I can't imagine that many people.

So I did it four or five more times and it started to get horrible. The show wasn't bad, but the hours were midnight to 5 a.m. I was doing the morning show at KCMO, so it was like I was staying up twenty-four hours straight. They said, "Well, we'd like to have you stay on. We're not sure when Art'll be back." I said, "No, sorry. I just can't do it."

I did learn one thing from doing the Art Bell show. From all the callers that come in, from all the cities, Kansas City, New York, Los Angeles, the callers that caused me the most problems were from San Francisco. I don't know, maybe things get weird there at night, but they all seemed to think they were superior to everyone else.

KANSAS CITY'S FIRST ST. PATRICK'S DAY PARADE

This is kind of an historic day for me in many ways. I'm telling this story on St. Patrick's Day 2008 from the Salty Iguana, where they're serving green margaritas today.

This is the fortieth anniversary of my coming to Kansas City. I came to here in 1968 and the first person I met was Len Dawson and the second person I met was Jim Lynch, All-American hero for Notre Dame who played in what's been called "The Game of the Century."

In 1966, Michigan State, coached by Duffy Daugherty, had an undefeated 9-0 record and was ranked Number 1; Notre Dame, coached by Ara Parseghian, was undefeated with an 8-0 record and ranked Number 2. The game ended in a 10-10 tie. It can't get much closer than that.

Anyway, Jim was number 51 for the Kansas City Chiefs, one of their all-time great linebackers. We were both working at KMBZ and he said to me, "You like Notre Dame?" I said, "Oh, my God, I've spent my life rooting for Notre Dame." Then Jim said, "I'm gonna take you to a place and introduce you to a man you're going to love." I said, "Who's that?" He said, "You'll see."

And he took me down to Hogerty's Saloon on Baltimore and I met Dan Hogerty, who looked like Santa Claus, and was every bit as jolly. He was in his upper sixties, he had snow white hair, weighed about 250, was about five foot six or seven, with a beautiful face.

Dan said he had a son at Notre Dame, Dennis, and we all sat down and talked about football and life and Kansas City and Notre Dame. And after a while, I started going down to Hogerty's every day after I got off my show at KMBZ.

I'd get off at 10 a.m. and go on down to Hogerty's and hang out with people. That's where I met one of my other great friends, an advertising guy named Pat O'Neill. So Dan and Jim Lynch and Pat and I wound up spending almost a year getting together every day at Dan's saloon.

One day on St. Patrick's Day, I was sitting with Dan and Pat and I said, "Look out there. It's St. Patrick's Day and there's not a soul on the street. There's no celebration, no party, no anything. Next year I'm gonna do a parade." Dan and Pat said, "That won't work in this town. People won't support it, they won't go to it or anything." I said, "I don't care. Next year I'm gonna give it a shot."

Dan Hogerty had a daughter named Kelly, and Kelly was married to Cy Perkins, who became another one of my greatest friends. And so the next year, I told Cy, I said, "We're gonna do this thing for your father-in-law, Danny. We're gonna start a parade. We'll start at the Continental Hotel and we'll walk down Baltimore and we'll end at Hogerty's Saloon and get Dan some business, because there just isn't anything going on down there on St. Patrick's Day." And he said, "That'd be great."

So I started talking it up around the first of March and I figured when St. Patrick's Day rolled around there'd be plenty of interest. So on that day, Cy met me outside the Kansas City Club and we'd been talking about it for weeks, and I said, let's go up to the Continental Hotel and see if anybody shows up.

So Cy and I walked up to the Continental Hotel and there was nobody there. Nobody. Just Cy and me. He looked at me and he said, "This is really embarrassing. This is really tragic." We stood there on the corner for about half an hour. Finally Father Hart, Father Jim, and Father Joe brought the first grade class from St. Regis School and they came. Then Hogerty and Jim Lynch got there and Mike Bonahan from Gigi's Bar joined us. Hogerty was wearing a handmade sandwich board sign that said, "The Parade Starts Here" on the front and "The Parade Ends Here" on the back.

So there was Cy and Jim Lynch and Carl J. DiCapo from the Italian Gardens and Dan and the priests and the kids… maybe thirty of us. And we started off walking from the Continental Hotel and when we got to Hogerty's, we made a hard left and went in.

And Officer Bill Cahill of the Kansas City Police Department said, "I'm gonna stop the traffic here." And he cordoned off Baltimore, and the kids from St. Regis School started dancing in the street and we got quite a crowd to gather round.

All of a sudden the *KC Star* showed up – that was when they still had an evening edition. And they did a whole front-page story with Dan Hogerty's picture on it. It said "First Parade in 100 years in Kansas City." And it came out late that afternoon. The block and a half parade was billed as "the world's shortest and worst parade."

But hundreds of people showed up for what became a downtown street party. Dan went out and got a paper and brought it back into the bar and he said, "Mike, this is the first time I've had this much business in my whole life." And he looked at it and got tears in his eyes and he said, "Look at me. I'm a saloon keeper and I'm on the front page of *The Kansas City Star*."

That began one of the greatest friendships I ever had. And it also kicked off the first Kansas City St. Patrick's Day Parade. That happened in 1973… exactly thirty-five years ago this very day.

A MAN CALLED RICHARD HARRIS

We used to watch a lot of talk shows. I always thought Jack Paar was the best. He'd come out there and sit on that stool and talk about his wife and daughter, Miriam and Randy.

Of the people who used to make the rounds on the talk shows, Richard Harris was one of my favorites. What a great talent. Whenever he came on a show you knew there was gonna be fireworks. Nine times out of ten he'd wind up getting up and walking off. I guess he had a low tolerance for dumb interview questions.

So it came to pass that he was booked in Kansas City. And he was supposed to come on my show. But before my show, he was supposed to go on Channel 5's *Noon Show*. So when the people came down from doing the *Noon Show*, they said, "Don't have him on today. He just walked off the *Noon Show*. He's in a bad mood and there's no way any good can come of this. He's gonna get you!" I thought, "Man, he's not gonna get me. I know I can do this."

So I got to thinking what I could do and I went to my producer and said, "Get me a copy of 'MacArthur Park' and when he walks in the door, hit it." Well, Richard Harris walks in the studio and "MacArthur Park" starts playing, and he sits down and looks at me and he doesn't say a word. And that beautiful song is playing and when it gets to that musical bridge, he starts playing with his fingers on the table like drumsticks. So we're both sitting there and he's drumming with his fingers and we played the whole thing. I never said a word to him.

When he was done, he looked at me and I looked at him, and I said, "That's one of the best pieces of music that's ever been recorded. How did you do it?" And he told me how the recording went, with Jimmy Webb, the writer and producer. And how he had to blend his voice with a female singer to hit that high note at the end.

And I knew right then we had a chance to get on good terms. So the first thing I asked him was, "Have you ever been to Durty Nellie's?" He looked me in the eye and said, "What do you mean have I ever been to Durty Nellie's? I had my first drink in Durty Nellie's." (Durty Nellie's is an old, seventeenth-century Irish pub in Limerick, Ireland. It's right next to Limerick Castle and full of Irish history, Irish music, and Irish people, always having themselves a good a time as can be had on this planet.)

Well, now we're just thicker than thieves. Of course Richard's an Irish guy, born and raised right there in Limerick. So he stayed for an hour, hour and a half, and we talked about everything from rugby to acting to movies to music to life and love. It was one of the best interviews I ever had.

The kicker to this story is that Richard Harris had met Jimmy Webb somewhere outside of Los Angeles and they were driving along in a car headed down the coast highway. Jimmy Webb was telling Richard Harris, "I'm gonna do this new song I wrote and I want the Fifth Dimension to do it." The Fifth Dimension had won a Grammy the year before with Webb's "Up, Up, and Away."

So Jimmy started humming the new tune to Richard as they drove. It was the haunting melody of "MacArthur Park." He told Richard he had almost got the deal signed for the Fifth Dimension to record it. And as they're driving along, Richard sees this piano sitting on the patio of one of these houses with all the glass in the back. Well, Richard was driving and he said, "Let's go up to that house. I want to do something." So they pull in the driveway and they walk up to the door and knock. When it opens, Richard says, "Hello, I'm Richard Harris and this is Jimmy Webb. I wondered if we could borrow your piano for a few minutes."

The people recognized Richard and said, "Sure, come on in." So Richard asked Jimmy to play that new song on the piano. I think Jimmy had a piece of paper with the lyrics written on it. And Richard started to sing. After a few bars, Jimmy Webb looked at Richard and said, "Mr. Harris, you've got yourself a deal."

THE SHOE STORE

You know how they say just a minute or two can make a world of difference? Like if you leave home at two minutes of seven o'clock and you get where you're going just fine, but if you'd have left home at two minutes after seven o'clock, you'd have been broadsided by a semi truck? And how one thing happens that affects your whole life, but you never know it at the time?

I came home to work at Nelson's Shoe Store, where I'd worked in high school. The way I got the job in the shoe store was from a guy who used to drive us back and forth from high school. The guy's name was Gene Kerwin and he worked at the shoe store washing windows with a squeegee and he said to me one day, "Look, you want my job? I'm getting a new one." And I said, "Sure." So I went down to Nelson's and interviewed with a man named Lenox Hummel and he said, "Yeah, you can work here. Start next week." So I think I was fifteen or fourteen.

So I started working there washing the windows every night, and trimming the windows once a week on Thursday night and selling shoes on Saturdays.

One day a man came in and he said, "I want to buy a pair of Florsheims." And I said, "Great!" He said, "You know, you have a good voice. How'd you like to be on radio?" I said, "Well, I'll give it a shot." Well, that didn't work out, but the seed was planted. And the reason I'm telling this story is if it wasn't for Gene Kerwin getting me that job in the shoe store and that guy coming in to buy a pair of Florsheims, I'd have probably never thought of broadcasting and had the career that I did. Thank you, Gene Kerwin.

THE QUEST FOR THE GLADSTONE

I don't know how I pulled this off, but after our successful "invasion" of Paola, Kansas (based, in a nutty way, on the "Payola Radio Scandals"), I started looking around for other crazy things to do. I started calling myself "El Murpho the Searcher" and wondering what weird things we could do with different towns in the area.

I went to station management and I said, "You know, there's a little town over here, north of the river, called Gladstone. Wouldn't it be something if there was an actual Gladstone, made out of stone, somewhere in the world, and I could go get it and bring it back here for the people in that town up there." They said, "Where do you think that'd be?" And I said, "I think it'd have to be in Ireland."

In those days, when my ratings were still through the roof, I could sell management on anything. So they said to go ahead. And Cathy and I get on a plane and we fly to London and we get into Heathrow Airport. Here we are, a couple of kids from Ottumwa, Iowa, who've never been anywhere and now we're in London, England.

We get a cab to take us to the city and all you can see are chimneys. Most of the places over there don't have central heating, so the people heat their homes with lots of fireplaces scattered around, and where you've got fireplaces, you need chimneys. It was like that scene from Mary Poppins – the "Chim-chimeny" song with Dick Van Dyke dancing on the roofs.

I was really taken with the city of London because it was so big. It just seemed to go on and on, from one neighborhood to the next. It was really neat. And when we get to the hotel, it was the Flemings on Half Moon Street, and that night we went out and had a little something to eat. I remember there were no street lights and I could see Jack the Ripper jumping from roof to roof – one of those kinds of nights.

The next morning we went into the coffee shop and there was another guy in there who sounded Irish and we asked him where he was from and he said, "I'm from County Cork, Cork City." So we started talking to him and he said, "What are you doing over here?" And I said, "We're going to Dublin and be in their St. Patrick's Day parade." I said, "What are you doing here?" He said, "Well, I don't like to be in Ireland on St. Patrick's Day so I come to London."

He told me his name, which was Alan Navratill. We had a nice visit and he said, "When you get to Ireland, give me a call and we'll get together again."

So we leave London and fly to Ireland, to Dublin. We get another car and go to our hotel, which was the Russell Court Hotel in Dublin City, an old hotel located on St. Stephen's Green. Now remember, we're on a mission to find a Gladstone. And when we walked into the bar, there were a bunch of pictures of people over the top of it and believe it or not, one was a man named "Lord Gladstone."

I thought, "This is just too weird. Here I am on a mission to bring back a Gladstone to Gladstone, Missouri, and here's this guy over the bar in Dublin named Lord Gladstone."

We had a real nice time there that night. It was March 16, and I was gonna be in the Dublin St. Patrick's Day parade the next day. Toward the end of the night, a cute little old man, who looked like a hotel bellhop, came up to me and said, "Mr. Murphy? Would you like to come into the bar and have a drink with me?" And I said, "Yes, I would." He said, "You know, you can drink all night as long as you're a resident of the hotel.

I'll just stay with you and keep the bar open as long as you want."

I said, "What could be better than this?" So Cathy went up to the room. We'd had one of the best meals I'd ever had. And when we got into the bar, he said, "Now sit down and I'll bring you something." He had a beautiful Irish accent and he looked just like Barry Fitzgerald in the movie, *Going My Way*.

His name was Paddy O'Rourke and he said, "Sit down and enjoy yourself. I'm here as long as you're here."

So about three in the morning I said, "I've got to go so I can get up for the parade tomorrow." He said, "Okay, if you're sure. I could stay longer." I said, "No, I'd like to stay but I've really got to go."

I wanted to give him some kind of tip for all his kindness so I said, "Do you have any money?" He said, "Let me show you." He opened his billfold and the only thing he had in it was a bus token to get home. No money at all. He said with a smile, "This is all that I've got to get me home. This'll have to last me till tomorrow when I can get another token from me wife."

So I gave him a really huge tip and he started to get teary eyed. He said, "You know this is the best time I ever had in my life just talking to you and now you give me this tip that will buy me bus tokens for months." As we were saying good night he also told me that I'd spent more money in that place than anyone else except the Queen. It made me think that the Queen must really know how to party.

But I loved spending those hours with that wonderful little man who looked and sounded just like Barry Fitzgerald.

The next day we went to Kilkenny Castle. We had called ahead and had the "Gladstone" cut and ready to receive.

It was an amazing surprise. I was greeted by the mayor of Kilkenny and a dozen Kilkenny councilmen. The mayor had me kneel in front of her and she took her sword and touched my shoulders and said, "Arise, Sir Michael Murphy, now a Knight of Kilkenny."

PIZZAZZ

When I was a kid I was crazy about horses and dogs. I wound up owning a horse, but this story is about collies. I always wanted a collie. That was, of course, from my love of the movies and *Lassie Come Home* and all the great Lassie movies.

I just thought they were the most gorgeous dog in the world and I always wanted one. When I was a kid I had cocker spaniels, and they are wonderful, loving dogs. But I never had a "Lassie" collie dog. So one day after I was just married, I said to my wife, "Let's go buy a collie. I saw an ad in the paper." She said, "No, we can't have one. We don't have enough money to eat ourselves." So I said, "I'll tell you what, I'll quit drinking Scotch if we can get a collie." And she said, "Okay." So this old lady named Dorothy Ridge had a bunch of collie pups for sale and we drove out to her farm. We walked up to the farmhouse and saw this huge collie named "Chief." It was just gorgeous. Mrs. Ridge said, "I have one here that's not too good but I'll sell it to you cheap." And so we bought the dog and took it home. And it wasn't much good. It wound up getting hit by a car. So I said, "Let's get some more." So we went back to Mrs. Ridge and said, "Poor old Mack, he got hit by a car and died." Then she said, "I've got two more and they're really good." And so we bought the two and raised them. But they weren't really show dogs and I was starting to get really into it. I wanted something really classy. Show dog material.

There was a man named Steve Fields in Omaha who had Parader collies, and I called him and said, "I want to get the best dog you've got." So he said, "I've got a couple of good ones now. Why don't you come on out." So we went out to Omaha and bought a female that was pregnant by a champion. We said we'll take that one. So we took her back with us and we ended up moving to Indianapolis. And there she gave birth to this litter of pups. We sold 'em and we made some money and that was nice.

Then we found another breeder in Indianapolis and her name was Mrs. Sterm, and she had the best looking collies I ever saw in my life. And they were called Lick Creek…the Lick Creek line of collies. And we went to her house and met her and talked to her and she said, "I'd like to breed with your dog." So we did. She had a champion named Champion Drummer Boy, and we bred the two and it produced a litter, one of which she took for her own for the breeding fee and she named him "Pizzazz." She called us about ten years later and she said, "Do you know whatever came of Pizzazz?" And I said, "No, what?" And she said, "Pizzazz became the greatest show collie that's ever lived. It won more championships and sired more champions than any collie in history." Even Lassie couldn't do that!

BARRY GOLDWATER'S SECRET

Somehow all this flying saucer business seems to tie itself together. In the early 1990s, the president of the Phoenix Chamber of Commerce came on the radio show one morning as a guest.

I used to go to Phoenix a lot so I said to him, "I'm coming down there in the spring. We used to go to a horse track down there, Turf Paradise. and we always have a great time in Phoenix. I love Phoenix." Kansas City people always like going to Phoenix. So the president of the Phoenix Chamber of Commerce said, "When you come down, look me up and we'll go have lunch." Then I said, "Listen, could you by any chance set up a visit for me with Barry Goldwater?" He said, "You know, I actually know Barry's brother, Bob. I'll bet I can line that up."

So I got down to Phoenix in February and I called him and he said, "It's all set. I'm gonna take you to Bob's house, then he's going to go on and take you up to Barry's house." So we went to Bob's house, which is adjacent to the Phoenician Hotel and Golf Course. And if you remember Charles Keating of the "Keating Five," the group that helped bring down the savings and loan business, well, they built the Phoenician Hotel with savings and loan money. The swimming pools were lined with mother-of-pearl and there were million-dollar pieces of artwork everywhere. It's just a fantastic place. So anyway, we get in Bob's car and drive up to Barry's house and go in and there's this old man sitting at his desk looking out over the valley and then I'm sitting down with him and it's Barry Goldwater.

It was a time I'll never forget. He visited with me for about an hour. When I got back to the hotel I didn't want to listen to the tape because I was afraid it wasn't any good. But after about a week I got it out one night and I played it and I think it's the best thing I ever did…sitting there with that old gentleman, talking about his life and his career and what he was thinking about. Anyway, he told me his story about the Roswell flying saucer crash. I'm not sure he ever told anyone else. Arizona and New Mexico had always been "hot spots" for flying saucer sightings and I asked him if he knew anything about the Roswell crash in 1947. He smiled a big smile and said one time he actually called his old boss in the Air Force, General Curtis LeMay, who was also his best friend, and asked him if he'd ever heard the rumor about a UFO from Roswell being taken to Wright-Patterson Air Force Base in Dayton, Ohio. He said to the general, "Curt, I hear you have some stuff over at Wright-Patterson that they found at Roswell and I'd like to get in there and see it if I could." Curtis LeMay told him, in no uncertain terms, "Don't ever mention this topic again to anyone, ever! End of conversation."

That tape has gotten worldwide attention. I was on the Art Bell show and he said, "Can I have a copy of that?" So I sent him a copy and he's often played it on his nationally syndicated all-night show.

ANDREW YATES

When I was a kid my mother used to listen to Mike Murphy and so I decided, as a young boy going to college, this is who I would listen to. Every afternoon I'd get out of school about two o'clock and turn on the radio to Mike's show. He played this incredible piece of music, the fanciest thing I'd ever heard. So one day while he was on, I called the show and I said, "What's the name of that song?" He said, "It's called 'Ballet in Brass' by Vic Schoen." I said, "Can I borrow your record?" He said, "Sure, come on down to the station and I'll lend it to you."

So I drove down to the radio station -- this is when it was in Fairway, Kansas. I borrowed the record and I copied every page of liner notes from the album jacket and then I dubbed the music onto a cassette tape. I loved this piece of music.

So I called the New York musicians' union and said, "Do you have a Vic Schoen listed?" They said no, try Los Angeles. So I called there and they said, "He's moved to Cripton, Washington." So I called this guy out of the blue and I said, "Hello Mr. Schoen. This is Andy Yates and I'm calling from Kansas City. I was listening to a record of yours called Stereophonic Suite for Two Bands. *It's the most incredible thing I've* ever heard and I'd like to see the music for it." He said, "Sure, I'll send it to you if you promise to return it." And that began a relationship with Vic Schoen that I value to this day.

So in the year 2000, I was working for the Royals Radio Network and they were about to bust up the department and I got a phone call that said, "You wanna be Mike Murphy's producer?" I said, "Sure!" And I came on the air with him July 20, 2000, and the first song I played on the air with him was "Ballet in Brass." And I had come full circle with that piece of music with Mike Murphy. It just shows you what one piece of music can do to your life.

I stayed with Murphy for four and a half years and it's the best four and a half years I ever had in my life.

This is the story of how we came up with our famous "Liberty Fanfare" opening we used in the show. In the year 2000, when I became Mike's producer, we used to use these goofy little openings for the show that I'd dig up here and there. But after September 11, I was on vacation and I was supposed to be in New York September 12 because I was taking my son on a trip. But because of what happened, we canceled our trip and I had the week off.

When I returned to work on the next Monday, we played one of those goofy openings, and after the show, Mike took me to lunch at the Hereford House out at Town Center. He said, "You know, I want to use something different to open the show now, something not so goofy. This just isn't the right time for it. Maybe something with a little more patriotism involved. Not the national anthem, but something with a little more power. Over the top of it I'd like to use that five-word opening from the old Ben Casey show, 'Man. Woman. Birth. Death. Infinity.'"

The reason we used that was six months prior to September 11, we had done a program called, "Your Favorite Television Show Theme Songs."

One of the theme songs I played that day was the Ben Casey theme and Mike liked to hear those words, "Man. Woman. Birth. Death. Infinity."

So Mike said, "I want you to come up with a new piece of music and I want you to use: Man. Woman. Birth. Death. Infinity."

So I had suggested "Liberty Fanfare" by John Williams several months ago and Mike said he didn't like it "because there's a slow part in that that doesn't belong." So that evening, I went home and put on the "Liberty Fanfare" again and dumped the slow part and brought in this faster section that we liked. And every time the chimes played, we'd say one of the words.

Mike said, "That's great, but I also want you to add a gong when those chimes ring." I said, "Sure." And I added a gong and when we played it, it was really emotional to hear.

After about six months, Mike was on the air and said, "I think we're gonna change this theme song. Try something new." And the emails and the phone calls came in droves and said, "Don't you touch that! Don't change a thing." So we used that till the day of the last show at Kelly's.

One other thing. In 2004, Memorial Day weekend, they were having a concert at Liberty Memorial with the Kansas City Symphony. And before the next song was played, the conductor turned to the audience and said, "This is the 'Liberty Fanfare,' written by John Williams, to commemorate the rededication of the Statue of Liberty in 1986. Or, as most of you know it, 'The Theme from the Mike Murphy Show.'" There was even a news reporter walking through the crowd, and when the song came to the gong part, people in the audience were going, "Man. Woman. Birth. Death. Infinity."

L.A. AND CARYL CHESSMAN

I went to L.A. for a week to do the show – or many shows – from the studios of KISS, where Rick Dees was working. He was so big back then. Remember the "Disco Duck"?

But the first guest I wanted to have on was Steve Allen. So Steve said, "I'll do it. I know Murphy and I love him." I also wanted to get the former governor of California, Pat Brown. There had been this huge protest about the execution in the gas chamber of a guy named Caryl Chessman. He was known as the "Red Light Bandit." He had been on death row for twelve years and had become kind of a folk hero. He had always proclaimed his innocence and there were constant protests on his behalf.

Steve Allen was against the death penalty and, ironically, so was Governor Brown, who had granted him many stays of execution. Steve had led a parade of people who burned candles and went to the prison every night. Finally the appeals ran out and Pat Brown said this was the hardest decision he ever had to make.

All of this had happened in 1960, years before I had them in the studio that day, and it seemed like Steve and Governor Brown had never really met or talked about it afterward. It was quite a coup. Great points of view from either side. And the only people who heard it were in Kansas City. I was at KISS in Los Angeles, but they just beamed it back here for my Kansas City audience.

CHARLES GUSEWELLE

I wanted to do a chapter about my favorite guests, but then I decided I couldn't do that, because there wouldn't be a favorite guest or a least favorite guest, except David Ogden Stiers, the worst guest I ever had.

But one of my favorites is Charles Gusewelle, without whom this book would not be possible. He's the guy, dear friend, who suggested to *The Star*'s book division that I should do a book.

One day I was having lunch with Charles and I showed him this rough layout that Steve had put together for me to give people an idea of what the cover of the book might look like. Charles said, "Look, I'm meeting with the Star Books people tomorrow. Have Steve fax me a copy of this cover and I'll bring it with me and show them."

Well, he did that and they said, "Sure, we'd like to do that with him." So this book which you're reading probably would not have happened without him. In fact I'm sure it wouldn't have.

But Charles would come on with me many times. And we had great visits, great talks.

But one that I remember is that I was going to St. Louis, and Charles was one of the last guests I had on before I went to St. Louis for my ill-fated St. Louis escapade. And I didn't have a car that day, and Charles said, "I'll take you home."

So we got into Charles's old car, and it started to sleet. His windshield wipers wouldn't work, and so there we were. It was dark and it was winter. And I thought we're gonna wreck here, and it's gonna be not only the end of my show, but the end of me, too.

And Charles.

The windshield wipers didn't work and the heater didn't work, and there we were. And he said, "Can you put your head down low and look through the windshield and kinda guide us and tell me to go left or right." So that's the way I got home with Charles. We sat there at our house and had a great visit.

It was, I think, that night that I decided I'd made bad mistake and I shouldn't go off to St. Louis. And matter of fact, I tried to get out of the deal, but I couldn't at that point, but Charles is certainly one of my best friends and one of my all-time favorite guests.

OTTUMWA COUNTRY CLUB

When I was a kid, around twelve or thirteen, of course I had to work. And one of the jobs you could get was to caddy at the golf course with the rich guys. So I'd go out there and caddy and carry what we called "doubles," one golf bag on each shoulder. It was called Ottumwa Country Club and the bankers and lawyers and doctors would come and we'd carry both their bags for eighteen holes. And they'd pay you like two bucks, maybe three. And I guess that was pretty good back then and so that's what we did.

Sometimes you'd follow these bankers and lawyers and doctors into the clubhouse when they were through. It was about a hundred degrees. And they'd sit down and order Miller Beer – "The Champagne of Bottled Beer." They'd drink it and it was cold and you could just imagine how good it must have tasted. But the caddies weren't allowed in there. We weren't allowed in any part of the country club.

So now, it's fifty years later and I go back and I go to that same country club and I'm sitting at the bar and I said, "When does the dining room open so you can order some food?" They said, "No, I'm sorry, but you're not gonna be able to eat here."

And I thought, "How are they gonna remember me from fifty years ago, when I was a caddy and couldn't come in the clubhouse… how could that be?" So I said to the lady, "You don't remember me or know who I was or anything. I used to caddy here, but surely the old rules don't apply still?" She said, "No, the kitchen's closed today."

I'm thinking, "Some things never change… even when they do."

OTTUMWA RADIO

Back in Ottumwa when I first started in radio, in 1958, I was working mornings at the radio station, KLEE. I had to go in real early and then fall back asleep. So Cathy would call me there every morning and wake me up. She'd say, "Mike, the station's not on the air." You used to have to warm up all the tubes in the station before you started broadcasting, but I'd be late so I'd just start broadcasting and blow out all the tubes. The engineer would come in and say, "What'd you do?" I'd say, "I don't know. I warmed up the tubes. I don't know what happened." I always had trouble getting up in the morning. I don't know how I did morning radio for twenty years!

After I was at KLEE – 1480 on your radio dial — for about a year, a little man came to town. His name was Al Evans. He said, "I'm with Bill O'Connor, one of the greatest announcers in the country. And he's coming in to buy the station. But they've heard you and they want to take you out of here and bring you to Springfield, Illinois."

And Al turned out to be one of the best and funniest radio guys I've ever known. He'd dance and he'd sing and he'd call you at night while you were on the air and say, "Play me this record." He always liked a song by Toni Fisher called "The Big Hurt." It was a great song with an amazing arrangement.

All these years I've stayed in touch with Al. When he hired me to go to Springfield, he said, "I understand you're very young." I was nineteen. But he said, "Hell, I'm young, too. I'm not thirty yet." So that was almost fifty years ago. And I just talked to him again. And he said, "Mike, you know what?" And I said, "What?"

He said, "I'm gonna be eighty." And I thought, "Boy, the time went fast." We've kept in touch now for fifty years. What a business. Al Evans is one of the greatest guys I've ever known.

OMAR SHARIF

I was always fascinated with movies and I'm thinking of one of the biggest productions of all time with Omar Sharif and Peter O'Toole called *Lawrence of Arabia*. It won seven Academy Awards in 1963, it was nominated for eleven!

Omar Sharif was terrific in it and was nominated for Best Supporting Actor. Women were just fascinated with him for some reason. He was an Egyptian who also became one of the best contract bridge players in the world. He had a bridge advice column which ran in many papers.

So the producers told me, "You're gonna have Omar Sharif on next week," and I'm wondering, "How's this gonna go?"

So he comes in the studio and we sit down and we have a great time. And I said, "Tell me about making *Lawrence of Arabia* with Peter O'Toole." He said, "What do you want me to tell you?" I said, "Did you have any fun doing *Lawrence of Arabia*?" He said, "Fun?" He said, "We were out in the desert for a year! The only 'fun' came when they'd give Peter O'Toole and me a week off to go to some local town. And being in the desert that long, we'd worked up a powerful thirst. So we'd drink everything in sight: beer, whisky, martinis… whatever they had! And we'd stay drunk for the whole week and the movie company would have to come with nets to get us back on the set. It was just terrible in that desert with all that heat."

Later he made a movie that was set in Las Vegas about a guy who was a blackjack hustler and Omar was the "house man" and this guy was about ready to break the bank so they sent him in and he saved the casino from going broke. And while he was filming that, he was gambling in his spare time and he lost all the money he was paid to make the movie. I said, "How much did you get paid for the movie?" He said, "I don't know. It was a million-two or a million-three. I lost it all in that short time I was filming there in Vegas."

Then I said, "Tell me about Peter O'Toole." He said, "Peter and I became great friends during the filming of *Lawrence of Arabia*. He and Richard Burton and Richard Harris were great rugby fans and would have quite a time going to the matches and celebrating afterwards."

This interview with Omar Sharif has special meaning because one time when I was back in Ottumwa, Iowa, I turned the radio on to KCMO and they were playing one of these *Best of Murphy* shows, and there is my interview with Omar Sharif. And I thought, "Here I am in the town I was born in and I'm listening to my interview with world-famous actor and bridge player, Omar Sharif."

ONE SCARY NIGHT IN MOLINE

The most major memory of Moline was we were living in this old rented house and it was a terrible winter, snowing all the time. About eleven o'clock one Friday night we heard this noise on our back porch. I went to the back door to look and there stood a man who looked like Frankenstein with blood coming out of his head. I thought, "What is this? What the hell is going on here?" And he starts banging on the door like he's trying to crash through. It looked like the door was starting to give. Cathy was standing behind it with a cheese knife. This is the biggest, ugliest thing I'd ever seen. So Cathy called the cops and told them what's going on. They said, "You'll have two of the biggest cops you ever saw on your doorstep in three minutes." So the cops got there just as he crashed through the door and they were even bigger than he was. They got him and took him away and it turned out he'd escaped from a nuthouse. The deal was we were living in the house that he grew up in as a boy and he was coming back there to live. He was crazier than a shithouse rat. That was one scary night in Moline, Illinois.

Shortly after that we moved to Kansas City.

THE DUKE CAME CALLING

Who'd of thunk that I'd ever get a call in the middle of the night from "The Duke," John Wayne? And maybe not just one call or five calls. Or ten calls. I lost count.

It happened to me when the Duke went to Louisville, Kentucky, for the Kentucky Derby. Well my brother, Pat, was in Louisville doing a radio show, and he managed to get himself introduced and they hit it off like thieves.

So John Wayne and Pat went to a pub and my brother said to him, "My brother, Mike, is in Kansas City and he'd sure like to talk to you." Well, the phone rings at our house and I pick it up and say, "Hello?" And I hear, "Hello. This is the Duke, John Wayne. I'm in Louisville with your brother Pat, and we're just sitting at a pub enjoying each other's company." I asked why he was there and he said he had to be Grand Marshal at the Kentucky Derby that year and he just wanted to say hi. Then we hung up.

About an hour, or maybe two, later, the phone rings and I pick it up and say "Hello?" He says, "Hello again, it's the Duke!" I said, "Well, how ya doing, Duke. What are you up to?" And he said, "Well, I'm sitting here with your brother and we're having a little Kentucky bourbon. When I got here I asked them to find me a good table and a good bottle of whiskey and I'd stay all night."

So I said, "How long have you been there?" and he said, "Oh, a couple of hours." So I asked him what his favorite movie was and we chatted for a while, and then I said, "Well, it's been nice talking to you. Take care."

After about the fifth or sixth time John Wayne called, I got to thinking, "Here I am, a mediocre disk jockey in a Midwestern town, and I'm being called almost every hour, by possibly the greatest motion picture star of all time." Maybe "the greatest that ever was or the greatest that ever will be," like Roy Hobbs in *The Natural*, one of the great sports movies of all time. The next time he called, I tried to make some conversation. I said, "Where are you staying in Louisville?" He said, "Those jokers booked me into the wedding suite at the Brown Hotel in downtown Louisville. It's got a whirl-pool bath and a mirror over the bed!

"Last night I went down to the bar and drank about a fifth of Jack Daniel's, then I came back up to the room and went to sleep. I woke up about three in the morning and looked up and I thought I was being attacked by a naked skydiver!"

Now the phone rings again. They've been in this tavern for hours now and he's feeling no pain. He says, "Hey, this is John Wayne. How ya doing, Pilgrim? We've been sitting in here since about three o'clock and things are really going well!"

Well, the Duke wasn't making a lot of sense so we hung up and I figured that was that. But, of course, it wasn't. The phone rings again at midnight and all I hear is, "This is the Duke calling." I said, "Hi again, John, how ya doing?" and all I hear is, "Da-buh rabba labba shump." I couldn't make most of it out. I could hear Pat in the background singing.

So I said, "Well, John, I just want to tell you again how nice it's been to talk to you." And he said, "Same here." And that was that. Or so I thought.

But now it's about two o'clock in the morning and the phone rings again! I can't believe either of them is still conscious. I say, "Hello?"

He says, "It's the Duke…" and then rambles on in gibberish for about three minutes.

John Wayne and my brother, Pat, are in Louisville and they're totally gassed and it's two in the morning. This is about the eighth call I've gotten that night, but I figure that's kind of a compliment that John Wayne calls you, not just once, but eight times in the one day. I'm sure he only remembered the first three or four.

But it was an honor, indeed, whatever condition he was in, to talk to the Duke one night, all night, on the eve of the Kentucky Derby.

John Wayne… the Duke came calling.

BASS WEEJUNS

In the mid-1980s, the station said they wanted me to have the man from Bass Weejuns in Ireland on the show. I said, "I don't know if I can talk about shoes for an hour." But he came on and we wound up talking about Ireland and we had a great time.

I never took guests home, but we really hit it off so I said, "C'mon. You gotta go home with me."

We got to my place and I took him back to a room in the house where I had some pictures. He looked up on the wall and he saw this one picture that he started staring at. I said, "Who are you looking at?" He said, "That's my next door neighbor and the guy on the right is my barber and the other guy lives down the street…" and he said he knew every one of them. And he started to cry. He said, "Here I am five thousand miles away from home, and I come to your house and I look up on your wall and here is a photo of all these people I know from my home town. It makes me real homesick and I'm sure glad you brought me here."

The people in the picture were citizens of Kilkenny, Ireland, at the ceremony where I was knighted.

BIRDHOUSE AND ETERNITY

In Catholic school we were taught about mortal sin at a very early age. If you committed a mortal sin, you were condemned to hell for eternity. And eternity was defined this way: "If a bird flew off from its cage every billion years and whittled his beak on a mountain top, when he had whittled the entire mountain away, only *one second* of eternity would have passed." That's a long time. That is the time you will spend in Hell if you have one impure thought. Well, that kind of talk can scare the shit out of a young kid heading toward puberty. Remember, this is not to do it, but just to even think about doing it! Of course almost all of these thoughts had to do with "carnal desires."

So my buddy Birdhouse, best guy I ever knew, went to confession. We had to go. They forced us to go every first Friday. And whether or not you wanted to tell what you'd done or even thought, you still had to go. So Birdhouse went this one time. And then I see him heading back again. I said, "What are you doing?" He said, "I gotta go back." So I see him again, heading back for the third time within an hour. And I said, "What are you doing?" He said, "I've gotta go back again." I said, "Why are you doing this?" He said, "I kept having these impure thoughts as I was walking away so I had to keep going back!" At that rate, we all could've been going back twenty-four hours a day. It'd never end.

THE MONASTERY

Well, we got so hung up on this sin business that Birdhouse and I decided we'd be monks. We'd just gotten out of high school and we went to a Trappist monk monastery in Dubuque, Iowa – New Melleray Abbey. We hitchhiked there. We used to hitchhike everywhere. Back then, that was just the way a lot of us kids got around. Birdhouse and I hitchhiked to Omaha one time and ended up walking back during the night, all the way from Omaha to Red Oak, a total of fifty-three miles!

So anyway, we get to the monastery and Brother Joachim let us in and we sat there and had meat sandwiches in a cell on the floor. We stayed there about a week. And I thought, "Man, this ain't for me." So we left. But Birdhouse went back for a whole summer, never saying a word. Trappist monks never talk. They take those vows of silence. For their whole life.

You wonder about things like that. Here was me, who talked for a living my whole life. What if I'd become a monk and never said a word?

SISTER LOUISE

With all that Catholicism and mortal sin and Trappist monasteries and confessions, there was always Sister Louise. An absolutely wonderful person.

My mother used to tell people, "I couldn't have raised Mike if it wasn't for Cathy [my wife] and Sister Louise."

MOTHER MERZ

When I was in high school, back in Monsignor Walsh Catholic School for Boys, all of us always talked about sports, and our favorite thing to talk about was the Iowa Hawkeyes. The basketball team was pretty good, but our favorite thing to talk about was Iowa Hawkeyes football.

Now, in the late fifties they had great teams, great players, coached by Forest Evashevski. In 1957 and 1959 their team won the Big Ten Championship and went on to the Rose Bowl twice: they beat Oregon State 35-19 in 1957 and California 38-12 in 1959. One of the stars of those teams was a tight end named Curt Merz. He was a first team All-American and I became a huge fan of his.

Back then when a team won the Rose Bowl, they'd go on the old *Perry Como Show* and Perry Como would always introduce all the Rose Bowl players and I thought, "Boy, this is really something."

Anyway, it was during those years that I started going to the University of Iowa myself and I got to be on campus with all those stars... Curt Merz, Randy Duncan, Alex Karras, Kenny Ploen. They used to hang out in a bar in Iowa City called the Airliner, and I used to go there just to be around those guys.

I never met "Mother" Merz, but he was a true football star and a kind of hero of mine.

Then a few years later, when I got to Kansas City, I was becoming something of a star myself. I knew that Mother Merz was here because he'd retired from the Kansas City Chiefs and he was working at the End Zone, one of the great bars in this town. It seemed like he was just bussing tables and stuff and I thought, "Boy, what is the deal?" So I asked my friend, Ed Lothimer, who owned the End Zone, "What's the deal with Mother Merz?" He said, "Well, he just comes in here to work a couple days a week."

So one day I started talking to him about Iowa football and stuff and after a while he said, "You're doing real good on the radio. Maybe I could do something like that." Well, I asked a friend named Jack Elliot, who was in the business, to meet with Curt and he said, "Curt, meet me down at the station at five o'clock in the morning on Monday."

So Curt came on with me and did real well and we met Jack Elliot back at the End Zone and he said, "Curt, I want to do a sports show with you and we'll call it 'Curt Merz, All-American Sports' on WDAF." So I'll be damned if he didn't get Curt a job there.

At that time I was on KMBZ and we were killing WDAF in the ratings. And he had no listeners because we'd just swamped the station. One night Curt calls me, while he's on the air, and says, "Murphy, rescue me and get me outta here!" And so they called him in and said, "You can't be doing that." So I called Walt Lochman and said, "Let's hire Curt and bring him over here with us." And I was able to get him over to KMBZ with us and, by golly, he got pretty good. He was doing *Middays with Mother*.

So it's kind of funny the way life is. He went from being my hero in football to me being his hero in radio. And we got to be great friends.

STEVE ALLEN

My friend Pat O'Neill was one of the best friends I ever had. He was kind of my "agent." He went to *The Kansas City Star* one time and said, "You gotta do a story about Mike Murphy," and I wound up on the front page. He worked in advertising and he was also the booker at Starlight Theater and he was always helping me get guests for the show.

One year Steve Allen came to town but he'd said he wasn't gonna do any interviews. But Pat went up to him and said, "You'll really like Murphy. Why don't you do his show?" So this one morning, it was about 7 a.m. Steve comes in and sits down and says, "How long am I gonna be here?" I said, "Three hours." He said, "Oh, my gosh!" But we really hit it off.

He said, "You know what? I came to town and I don't have any shoes." He just had on some old sneakers or something. I said, "What do you mean you don't have any shoes?" He said, "They just forgot to put any shoes in my suitcase. I've gotta find some shoes." I said, "What size do you wear?" He said, "Thirteen triple-A." That is one very unusual shoe size, but I came on the air and I said, "I've got Steve Allen here with me and we gotta get him a pair of shoes. He wears size 13 triple-A."

About an hour later a guy shows up at the station and he says, "I got the shoes." Sure enough he came in and he had these long, narrow shoes. And Steve just went crazy. He said, "This is the funniest, best thing that's ever happened to me." He laughed that wonderful laugh of his, kind of a high-pitched giggle, and when you heard it you had to laugh yourself. So he put the shoes on right then and there and said, "Now I'm all set."

Steve Allen was one of the most talented people that've ever been in the broadcast business. He was a musician, a comedian, and a writer. He was the first host of *The Tonight Show* in September of 1954. He was a great jazz pianist and composer who wrote more than ten thousand songs, including "This Could Be the Start of Something Big." Over the years Steve and I remained friends. When I went to Los Angeles to do the show, Steve was the first guest I wanted to have on.

As Steve was leaving the studio that first day after I got him the shoes, he said, "You know, I've been interviewed thousands of times by hundreds of different people, and you're the best I've ever been with." And I thought, "That's the greatest compliment from the greatest talent of maybe anyone who's ever been in the broadcast business." What an honor.

THE ROADS NOT TAKEN

John Holliday

When I came to Kansas City, after I left Moline, the program director's name was John Holliday, who had the image of the map of India on his tongue. He told me a story about when he was in World War I, he had seen a Tibetan monk actually levitate himself and fly over a river.

I'd originally started in the 9 p.m. to midnight slot, but after a while they decided to try me in the mornings. The morning show was getting only about an 8 to 10 percent share of the listener market. But in almost no time the rating shot up to a 20. Then a 25, a 30, and a 40! Finally, we had almost 50 percent of the listening audience in Kansas City listening to our morning show. It was insane.

So Walt Lochman, the station manager, called me one day and said, "Let's go to lunch." I think Walt was the most empathetic man I've ever met. I loved him and at the same time I hated him. I'm sure he felt exactly the same about me.

So we went to the End Zone, the world's greatest restaurant/tavern down by the Plaza, scene of many stories and good times. Walt showed me the numbers that had just come in and he said, "You've got a 48 share!" And he started to cry. He cried a lot. He said, "The number two station only got a 10!"

So he's crying and I said, "What's the matter?" He said, "I thought you'd have a 50!"

Walt was the damnedest guy I ever met. We had more fun together. We were like partners in the success of this crazy show. We ate it, we breathed it, we slept it… it was all we thought about. We fought. We partied. We laughed. We cried. It was one of the greatest relationships I ever had in my life.

I'm positive one of the reasons for our success was that the station gave us almost total freedom to do whatever we wanted. To play whatever music we wanted, to say nutty things and dream up crazy ideas and promotions. I think people here, when they tuned into the show, they never knew what was gonna happen, who was gonna be on, what was gonna get said. And half the time neither did we.

Somebody once said about me, "Murphy is a man who wished upon a city and became a star." I always kinda liked that.

New York City

Walt and I had a falling out. I had just won Billboard Disc Jockey of the Year.

Jack Elliot was the program director at our competitor, WDAF, and he was trying to get me out of town. So when I went to New York, Jack came with me. Well, the night of the Billboard Awards, when I was supposed to go up and receive my honor, Jack said the guys from the record company have got tickets for us to go to the Stork Club to see the Supremes. He said, "Well, what do you want to do, go to the awards ceremony or go see the Supremes at the Stork Club?" So I said, "I think we gotta go see the Supremes."

So there I was, supposed to get this Billboard Disc Jockey of the Year award, but instead I'm going to see the Supremes. But it really was a heck of a show.

So Jack said he had a friend from Pittsburgh named Don Scheef who had just become the program director at WNBC in New York. Remember, he wants me out of Kansas City because I'm working for his competition and killing his morning show. So Jack said, "I have you set up to meet with the guys from NBC tomorrow to do a live on-air audition."

A guy named Perry Bascomb was the manager at WNBC and he said, "What you're going to have to do is go on the air tomorrow at 4 p.m. and do a live show." Well, one thing I'd done at KMBZ that was popular was to do a parody of all the radio farm shows up in Iowa. They're pretty funny. A guy comes on and says, "Now cows are twenty bucks and pigs are thirty bucks…" They were terrible shows unless you were a farmer, but I used to do them for fun on my show and get a few laughs. I'd put sound effects in them, cows mooing, pigs snorting, roosters crowing. ("Cows are thirty dollars - *MOOO*! Pigs are twenty bucks – *SNORT*!") It was a lot of fun.

So I went on the air live at 4 p.m. in New York City and did this farm show. I had the engineers find some of the sound effects I needed. So we did the show and they got about ten thousand complaints. People saying, "What are you doing?" "That's the worst thing I ever heard." But amazingly, NBC thought it was great and they called me into the office. They said, "We're going to hire you here at WNBC in New York to do nine o'clock to midnight and you're gonna be the next big star in New York radio. We'll pay you $100,000 a year."

Now, $100,000 a year back in 1972 was a lot of dough. They went on to say, "We've hired a guy named Don Imus to do mornings and Wolfman Jack is gonna do afternoons, Long John Neville will do all-nights. You're gonna be the next Ron Lundy." You might remember hearing Ron Lundy because in *Midnight Cowboy*, when John Voight is getting into New York on the bus, he has this transistor radio playing and it's Ron Lundy. John Voight says to the people around him, "That's New York City talkin', man!"

So I get back to Kansas City and I tell my wife, "We gotta go to New York City."

She said, "I don't know…" And I talked to the kids a little (they were about three, five, and seven) and they said, "Dad, I don't know. We like it here." So that was the end of New York City, but as I look back on it I probably should've gone.

Detroit

The offers were coming in like crazy and the next big one came from Detroit.

It was the year 1969, I think, that the Chiefs were playing the Jets in a game to go to the Super Bowl. I got to Detroit and a man named Ken Draper wanted me to go to work at a station named WCAR. And the kicker to that deal was that they'd buy me a house in Grosse Pointe, Detroit's poshest suburb, and offer me a pretty decent salary to boot.

They put me up at a fancy hotel downtown called the Ponchartrain. I looked out the window the first night I got there and there were police on the streets with dogs and lots of squad cars and I said, "Man, I don't know about this." But the next day I met with Ken Draper and he made me the formal offer. I said, "Let me think about it for a couple days."

So I got back on the plane. That was when TWA was based in Kansas City and most of them knew me and they'd always upgrade me to first class. I always got the royal treatment. So after a while the captain came on the intercom and said, "The Chiefs beat the Jets, 16 to 9, and they're going to the Super Bowl."

When I got home I realized how much I really liked Kansas City, so when the guy from Detroit called and asked if I was coming, I said no. He stayed on the phone for two hours trying to talk me into moving to Detroit. I kept saying no. Then he called the next night. And the next. He kept calling all week and I kept saying no.

He finally said, "Heard your show in Kansas City and it was the best thing I'd ever heard. I really wanted to get you here. I especially wanted to have that thing you called 'The Odd Squad.'" Which is something I talk about somewhere else.

Chicago

I guess it was the early seventies and two guys came in from Chicago named Tony Grimm and Bob Mooney. Tony Grimm was the national program director for a company called Westinghouse. Westinghouse had a great chain of stations – San Francisco, Chicago, New York.

So they asked me to lunch and we went to the Playboy Club. They said, "We've been in town for a couple of days listening to your show and we'd like to hire you to come to Chicago and work at WIND." WIND was a station made famous by Howard Miller, who was married to June Valley, a great singer from back in the fifties.

They said, "We want to bring you in here to do afternoons and we're hiring a guy named Robert W. Morgan to do mornings" – who at the time was the number one guy in Los Angeles at KHJ. So I went to Walt Lochman and said, "Walt, I gotta go to Chicago. I've always loved that city." And Walt said, "No, you can't. I'm not gonna let you out of your contract. We do a lot of business with Westinghouse and if you leave, I'll tell Westinghouse we'll cancel our business with them."

So I called the Chicago guys back and they said, "We don't care. We're staying in town till you figure some way to get out of the deal." And they called Westinghouse and they called Walt and it went round and round and they wound up staying in town for two weeks. But they never did get me out of it. And that became another sore point in Walt's and my friendship. Again, love/hate.

Christmas Eve with Walt

Around Christmastime, shortly after the Detroit debacle, Walt and I went to a restaurant called the Pavilion, down on Baltimore, because Walt said he wanted to talk about this deal. It was Christmas Eve. We started talking at noon and the next thing we knew it was five o'clock and we're still not home. We'd had more fun together, we'd laugh, we'd cry, we'd tell stories. We'd had some drinks, it'd been a long day and I said, "Walt, I've gotta get out of here." Now it's six o'clock at night on Christmas Eve and I go to a department store to buy stuff for Christmas. I'm pulling everything off the countertops: radios, razors, hi-fi sets, dolls, baseball gloves… And I get home at eight o'clock and say, "Merry Christmas!"

You know, I don't know how I did it. I did it for forty-six years. How can you do anything for forty-six years? Especially the radio business, which is one of the toughest, least secure businesses there is. Most people survive for only three or four years, if that long. The business now is so different from what it was. Back then companies like Westinghouse and Golden West and Storer would go looking for good talent for local radio. There was so much variety and so much innovation. And the talent was so good. A man I met named Hugh Heller came to Moline one time and he was the man who got Golden West with Gene Autry going. He came to town and said, "Mister, you're gonna be good one of these days. Not now, but just wait awhile. It'll come to you."

And about ten years after that a guy I met in Philadelphia called and he said, "Mike, it's time to come to San Francisco." I said, "Where?" And he said, "KSFO." Now that was the number one station in San Francisco. Some say it's the best station that ever was. And there's a man named Don Sherwood doing mornings who had about a 30 or 40 percent share. He had a convertible and he used to transport a cougar around with him. The animal, not the car. Well, he had the convertible and the cougar was in it and of course the cougar attacked the roof and tore the top of the car apart. It was a front page story in San Francisco.

But anyway, something else was going on and I couldn't go to San Francisco and I'm still here in Kansas City and I'm not sure why. Maybe it's this book.

JOHN McCAIN

In the 2000 presidential primaries, John McCain had just won the New Hampshire primary and he was on a roll. He came to town and came on the show.

We had a great visit. He's a very personable man, good sense of humor. I remember him saying that he wouldn't trade his five and a half years in captivity for anything. I said, "You mean, if you could have those years back you wouldn't take 'em?" He said, "Absolutely not."

I never quite understood that. But whenever I comb my hair in the morning, I think, "John McCain can't comb his own hair because he can't raise his arms high enough from the torture techniques they used on him."

But we had a great visit and at the end he looked me right in the eye and said, "Now Mike, if I win this thing, I want you to come and do your show from the White House. I guarantee we'll set it up and make it happen." I said, "Do we have this on tape?" They said they did. I said, "Okay, John, I'm gonna hold you to that." And with that he got up out of his chair and waved goodbye. That was my visit with John McCain.

So if McCain is elected, I'm gonna try to get another job for a week and call him up at the White House and see if he remembers that. I bet he would.

ROD McKUEN, ARA PARSEGHIAN, AND JOE MONTANA

I was in Hawaii one time, I guess in the seventies, and I was walking down the street real late one night on Kapiolani Boulevard – the main street in Honolulu – and this guy who was walking toward me looked familiar. I looked at him and it was Rod McKuen. I don't know how many people will remember who Rod McKuen was, but he had a couple of great hit songs and he's been called the unofficial poet laureate of the sixties and seventies. So I said, "Rod?" And he looked at me and he said, "Yeah?" I said "Rod McKuen?" He said, "*Yeah*!" And I said, "It's nice to meet you. I'm Mike Murphy from Kansas City." And he said, "Glad to meet you. Let's go in here and have some coffee." It was a little coffee shop called Kona Gold and he and I sat down around midnight and talked till about 1:30 in the morning. And it was just great. We talked about everything under the sun – well, at that time of night it would've been the *moon* – from music to movies to politics to people to poetry. We said goodbye and I never really met him again. It was just a chance meeting with one of the most famous singer/songwriter/poets of the twentieth century. But it just goes to show you how nice and friendly people can be no matter who they are or what they're doing.

Ever since I was a little kid in Ottumwa, Iowa, about five or six years old, we used to follow Notre Dame football because we were Catholics. There was great discrimination against Catholics in those days, back in Ottumwa, because we were so outnumbered by Protestants. So my mother was always trying to legitimize our religion. She used to say, "Now we gotta watch Notre Dame football today." Well, we didn't actually watch it because we didn't have TV, we had to listen to it on the radio. But back then, everybody would just sit around and look at the radio, so I guess you could say we were "watching" it.

My mother was a real character. Whenever Notre Dame would play a team like SMU or TCU, she'd say, "Notre Dame is playing SMU, the Catholics are playing the Protestants, and Notre Dame has gotta win." So from then on I've always been a big fan of Notre Dame football... and all their great coaches: Knute Rockne, Frank Leahy, Terry Brennan, Joe Kuharich. Maybe the greatest of all was Ara Parseghian. I was a great fan of his, and he had a quarterback playing for him named Joe Montana. I'll tell you about Joe Montana in a minute.

But one day I saw Ara Parseghian walking down the street in Kansas City and I said, "Mr. Parseghian?" And he said, "Yes?" I said, "My name's Mike Murphy and I've always been a huge fan of Notre Dame." And just like Rod McKuen he said, "Well let's go in this restaurant and have a little visit."

So we sat there in the Pavilion for about an hour and talked about all the old Notre Dame players and the great coaches and what it was like to be a coach at Notre Dame. What a great guy he was. And just like Rod McKuen, he was as nice as he could be.

But now back to Joe Montana. When Joe Montana was playing for the Chiefs, he came into Johnny Cascone's restaurant one night with his wife – and a *bodyguard*! And I said to one of the owners, who are good friends of mine, "Could I just please meet Joe Montana?" I was never one to have much idol worship for anybody, but if anybody would have had that it would have been Joe Montana. So the owner said, "Yeah, sure,

I'll go back and see what I can do." So he came back in a few minutes and he said to me, "Joe said he will speak to you on his way out." So on his way out, I got up and Joe stopped. I put out my hand and said, "How you doing?" And he said, "How you doing?" then shook my hand and turned and walked out.

I guess if there's a moral here, it's, "Some people have time to talk to strangers and even enjoy it, other people are always in a hurry."

In fact, there's *more* than a moral here. There's actually a funny little story.

You've heard the current phrase, "What goes around comes around"? Well, a friend of mine happened to be the realtor who sold Joe his house, situated on the eighteenth green of one of the swankiest golf course communities in South Kansas City. And (no accident?) the realtor's house was nearby. Well, as it turned out, the realtor's daughter would housesit for Joe and the family when they were out of town.

So one night, when the daughter was house sitting over there, my realtor friend called me and said, "Hey, you wanna take a tour of Joe Montana's house?" I said, "Sure," and over we went. Well, the inside of the house looked like something from the pages of *Architectural Digest* and when we got to the master bedroom, an evil little idea started forming in my head. I said to my wife, "Cathy, I bet not many people can say they've slept in Joe Montana's bed." So in we both crawled and had ourselves a nice little "sleep." We remade the bed just like it was, but I've always wondered if he had a "Goldilocks Moment" when he finally got home. "*Who's been sleeping in my bed?*" It was ME, Joe!

FRANK GORSHIN AND CLINT EASTWOOD

There's a really funny but weird story about Frank Gorshin. He was a terrifically talented guy who was in hundreds of movies and TV shows. He's probably best remembered as "The Riddler" in the Batman TV series of the sixties. When he started out he was one of the greatest impressionists going. I don't know if he could do as many voices as Rich Little, but he could rearrange his face so he could actually look like the people he was imitating. He could look so much like Kirk Douglas or Burt Lancaster or Boris Karloff it was hard to tell the difference. So I thought if there was anybody I'd like to talk to it'd be Frank Gorshin. So one day it happened. He came to town and I was able to get him on the show.

So he came into the studio and he took one look at me and said, "I've gotta get outta here." I said, "What?" He said, "I'm terrified. I'm scared to death and I can't do this." He yelled into the other room to the friend that brought him and said, "Get me outta here. I gotta get to a drugstore." And then he said to me, "I'm sorry but I gotta leave." And that was it. Frank Gorshin left, a guy I wanted to have on all my life and he was here about thirty seconds. I always wondered what the hell was wrong, what scared him and what he could have wanted at the drugstore, but I never did find out. Another of my life's great mysteries.

Speaking of Rich Little, I actually did have him on one time and he was just a marvelous guest. I asked him what was the best show he ever had. He said, "I did a show one night and I was doing Bing Crosby and he was sitting in the audience right down front. Somehow I got tripped up and I fell off the stage and right into his lap. Ol' Bing said, 'Well, Bippity, Boppity,' and Bing said it was the greatest tribute to him that'd ever been done." Rich doesn't get as much exposure as he used to because he told me today's audiences don't know half of the people he "does" and he can't do the younger ones like Tom Cruise or Brad Pitt. But still, he's known as the "Dean of American Impersonators" and he's got a pretty steady thing going with the Golden Nugget in Las Vegas.

Every year there used to be a local group that brought famous celebrities to Kansas City. I think it was called "Show-a-Rama" or something. Well, the year I'm thinking of they brought Clint Eastwood to town and Clint was a friend of my brother, Pat. They met in Tucumcari, New Mexico, when my brother was a disc jockey and Clint was still playing Rowdy Yates on *Rawhide*. He came over to my brother's studio here in Kansas City one night to hang out, watch him play the records and do the all-night show. Clint said to Pat, "You know, I've always wanted to do that DJ thing just to see what that was like." So my brother said, "Come on over here and sit down and play these records."

So Clint Eastwood sat with my brother and played records all night. He said, "You know, I really enjoyed doing this. One of these days, when I get into the movie business, I want to make a movie about this." And sure enough, he did. It was called *Play Misty for Me*, and it was one of the scariest movies I think I've ever seen. And Clint named the bartender in the movie after my brother. The bartender's name was "Murphy."

So anyway, back to the Show-a-Rama story. They brought Clint to town, and Clint, of course, knew my brother, remembered him, so when he got to town he called my brother and said, "Let's go out for lunch, my treat." So my brother and I met him downtown and he took us to the End Zone.

So we went there, my brother and Clint Eastwood and a couple of

Clint's press people and they had lunch and they had some drinks and all of a sudden the place started to fill up because the word had gotten around that Clint Eastwood was at the End Zone. So now there are about five hundred people packed into a joint that couldn't hold two hundred people, and the girls got up on the stage with him and all of a sudden the damnedest fight you've ever seen started. So Clint Eastwood snuck out the back door with his people and left the bill and they never saw him again. The bill was $895. So as far as I know, Clint Eastwood still owes somebody in Kansas City $895.

ARTHUR MARX

You would think that with all the people I had in the studio and visited with I would have gone to lunch or taken some of them home, but I rarely did. There were only two or three.

Arthur Marx, Groucho's son, and I became good friends, and I took him home one night and stood him sideways outside the front door out at Squirrel Manor, what we called my old house. He knocked on the door and when Cathy came to the door he was standing sideways and he looked just like Groucho. Of course, Groucho's been dead all these years.

And she said, "Who in the hell is that?" I said, "It's *Groucho's*… [PAUSE] son, Arthur!"

So he came in with his girlfriend. They sat up drinking brandy with us and talking about old times until three o'clock in the morning. He was a real good guy, and I continued to have him on from time to time.

MAN AGAINST DOG

I used to go to the Woodlands a lot. They had a horse track on one side and a dog track on the other. I started by going to the horses, but they didn't run but for a couple months a year. So after they left, I guess you could say I went to the dogs.

It was a lot of fun. I'd never been to a dog track before, but the greyhounds were beautiful animals and it was just a whole lotta fun, so we started going.

I'd look in the paper the next morning to see who won what, what it paid, and so on. Then one morning I was looking at the schedule and I see a dog named Mike Murphy who's running in a training race.

So I called somebody at the track and I said, "This is Mike Murphy the man. What's the deal with Mike Murphy the dog?" And they said, "Well, we've got a trainer that wanted to name a dog after you." And then they said, "You know what?" and I said, "No, what?" and they said, "He's the damnedest dog we ever saw. He's won nine races in a row. We've never had a dog do that in the training races. Nine races in a row."

So I get to thinking, "Hmm, I wonder if Mike Murphy the Man should race Mike Murphy the Dog?" I thought we could really have some fun with that. So I called them up and told them about my idea and they said, "Oh, yeah, let's do that!" And so we did a promotion: "Mike Murphy the Dog versus Mike Murphy the Man" in a match race. I had a trainer, "Texas" Bob Geigel, the great pro wrestler from Algona, Iowa. And the dog had a trainer, Bulldog Bob Brown, the great pro wrestler from Manitoba, Canada.

So we got it all going, all put together. I had to run a hundred yards and the dog had to run a loop around the track, maybe eight hundred yards or so.

There was a lot of promotion around town. The race would happen right in the middle of the night's racing session with a full crowd. I heard there was a lot of casual betting going on in the stands.

I've only worn my space suit that Cathy made me three times: 1) On World Contact Day on the roof of the Power & Light Building; 2) In the Mike Murphy Man Versus Dog Match Race; and 3) For the famous "Mike Murphy's Last Show" at Kelly's in Westport.

For this race, Cathy had also made me an alien head to wear, so the way I entered the track was in a limo with a sunroof and I was standing up through the roof with the alien head on and the space suit. It must have been quite a sight.

Randy Burch, the track announcer, said, "And now, coming out of the car is Mike Murphy… er, wait, what's that? That's an alien in there!" And we circled the track and when we stopped I took off the alien head.

We got ready for the race and they shot the starting gun and I start off with my silver space suit on. And here I am running down the track and I can see the dog running around the other side, but very fast. Everybody said the dog would beat me, but I said, "No, I'm not gonna let him win."

Well, as it turned out it was really close, a photo finish, and Mike Murphy the Man beat Mike Murphy the Dog. And I got the Man Versus Dog Winner's Cup. And the kicker is that this dog, that had won nine races in a row and then lost in his match race against Mike Murphy the Man, never won another race in his entire career.

DAVID SCHOENSTADT

One of the smartest men I ever met was a guy that came here from San Francisco named David Schoenstadt. In 1980 he bought a soccer team called the San Francisco Fog, but in 1981 he moved them to Kansas City and changed the name to the Kansas City Comets. They lasted for ten years and were a terrifically successful team with a big following and popular players. In fact, one time they drew more fans to their indoor soccer game at Kemper Arena than the Chiefs did at Arrowhead.

David always had a reputation for being real smart, and one day, when he was younger, somebody said, "If you're so smart, why don't you go to medical school and become a doctor?" And he bet him around $500. Well David went to medical school, got the degree, and I guess the $500. Who knows what it cost him to go to medical school?

So when he got to town, I met him and he said, "You remind me of a radio guy in San Francisco named Jack Carney. But I think you may be even better than him." Well that was nice of him to say that, but the really funny, ironic thing was that I wound up replacing Jack Carney at KMOX in St. Louis after he died tragically while he was taking a swimming lesson. He was only fifty-two.

After I came back from St. Louis, David opened a restaurant downtown and named it after me, called "Murphy's Landing."

He told me this story and he claimed it was absolutely true. You can believe it or not. I warned you that some of the stuff in this book might not be 100 percent true. But David told me he was in the war – World War II – in Germany walking through a small village. He was carrying an M-1 rifle and happened to have one of those big M-1 shells in his breast pocket over his heart. Well, as he was passing by a house, an old lady about six stories up hauled off and hurled a steel-covered Bible as hard as she could. The Bible hit him square in the chest, right on the pocket with the shell. And he swore to me, he said, "Mike, if I wasn't carrying that bullet in my pocket over my heart, that Bible would've killed me." End of story. He always swore it was true.

Another time David came to me and said, "I need to borrow a million dollars." I've heard of people coming to me and saying they wanted to borrow a hundred dollars, or a thousand dollars, or even ten thousand dollars. But I never had anyone come to me and say they wanted to borrow a million dollars. He said, "Can you help me?" I said, "How could I help you borrow a million dollars?"

He said, "I don't know. I have this business and I need a million bucks. I thought you might know somebody." Well, I remembered I'd gone out with a friend of ours who was with a company who did just that. Lend people large sums of money to start businesses. So I mentioned to him what David had asked me and I said, "Can you do that?" He said, "Sure, we do that kind of thing. Let's set up a meeting."

So he got with David, David told him his idea and my friend, Larry, loaned him the one million dollars. In a while, David called me one day and said, "I'd like to thank you for setting this thing up with Larry." I said sure, and we met in this bar on the Plaza and he gave me a check for $60,000! I said, "What is this?" He said, "That's a finder's fee for getting me the money." I said, "You gotta be kidding! All I did was set up a meeting."

So there you are. I started out just doing a favor for a friend and I wind up with a check for $60,000. I guess it just goes to show, nice guys don't always finish last.

NAURA HAYDEN

Arthur Marx was only the second guest that I ever took home. The *first* one was Naura Hayden.

Naura was a great old gal, one of the first guests I ever had on KCMO. She came to town promoting something called "The Dynamite Milk-shake," and she was giving all the profits to prisoners.

She'd been in *Bonanza.* She was Big Red, Hoss's girlfriend. She was great lookin' and she was also in *The Angry Red Planet*, a great old science fiction movie, made back in 1960.

So she and I got to be great buddies. And I took her home one night and cooked her a steak. She was a vegetarian, but she said, "Since you cooked it, and since it's your meat, I'll eat it."

And so we had a great time with Naura. And through the years she said, "I'm gonna make a movie and I want you to be in it." And she did. The movie was called *The Perils of PK*, with Dick Shawn and Sammy Davis Jr. More about that later. But she was one of the two or three guests I ever took home.

Naura had a book out. It was called *HOW TO SATISFY A WOMAN EVERY TIME… and have her beg for more!*

It came out in 1982 and immediately went to number one on The New York Times best seller list. It's been reprinted several times since then. And so I'd have her on and she'd say, "I wanna talk about my book." And I'd say, "No way! I'm not gonna talk about that damn thing."

My mother used to listen to me up in Iowa, and she'd say, "I like your show every day except when you have that Naura Hayden on." Well, the book went to number one, with or without me, and about a year later she re-released it, and it went to number one again! That was the first time in history that a book ever went to number one twice on *The New York Times* best seller list.

Naura Hayden. A great woman. And I hope to see her again down the road.

THE PERILS OF PK

I guess this was in 1981 or '82, maybe. I was at KCMO doing talk radio in the morning. One of the first guests I'd had on as a talk show host was Naura Hayden, whose movie career as an actress and director spanned the 1950s through the 1980s. She was in a lot of TV shows – *Bonanza, Gunsmoke, Surfside 6* – but her real claim to fame was that she starred in a cult movie from 1960 named *The Angry Red Planet*.

She had a couple of best-selling books and she was married to Gary Stevens, founder and general manager of Warner Brothers.

So over the years we kept in touch and I'd have her on from time to time and one day she called me and said, "I'm making a movie and would you like to be in it?" And I said, "Well, of course I would." She said, "It's called *The Perils of P.K.* and I am going to be P.K., and I've got a good part for you."

She told me the cast was going to be, among others, Sammy Davis, Jr., Professor Irwin Corey, Joey Heatherton, Dick Shawn (who I loved), Larry Storch, and Sheila MacRae, the widow of Gordon MacRae, a terrifically talented actress and a wonderful person. In fact Larry Storch and Sheila MacRae came into Kansas City to help premiere the movie and I had them both on my show in the morning.

While they were on the air, Larry Storch did Spencer Tracy and Sheila MacRae did Katharine Hepburn and it was one of the darnedest things I ever heard. What great talents they both were.

So anyway back to the movie. Naura called and said come to New York on such and such a day, so my wife, Cathy, and I went to New York and stayed at the old Barbizon Hotel around 63rd and Lexington. The Barbizon was once called "New York's Most Exclusive Hotel Residence for Young Women," with no men allowed above the first floor. There was a famous rumor that Grace Kelly used to "prance down the halls in her skivvies."

When we got there those days were long gone. They had a great bar there, but the first thing we wanted to do was go to Aqueduct racetrack out in Queens. An author I knew named Bill Alden met us in the bar and said he had a limo he'd let us use the next day to go to the track.

So the next day we head out to Aqueduct and the driver started telling us all these stories about World War II. And it turned out that he was the interpreter for Roosevelt and Stalin at the Yalta Conference. He had all these stories about Roosevelt, what he was like, what Stalin was like, and it was just one of those amazing surprises that happen in life that tell you no matter who you meet or what they're doing, they may have an amazing story to tell.

So the next day we get to this huge sound stage in downtown New York to film this movie and there are all these characters sitting around. They had pigs in boxes and chickens and geese… it was just like a zoo! But all the animals in the world couldn't have helped this movie.

One more thing about Dick Shawn. He was an incredibly talented person. His comedy was totally original and unique. He was always in demand – for movies, TV shows, late night talk shows. When you had Dick Shawn around you were guaranteed something nutty and funny was going to happen.

About ten years or so after *The Perils of P.K.*, he'd gotten real hot again and I think it was the Hollywood Bowl or someplace and he was really packing them in. So the day before one show he said, "Tonight I'm going to do something totally original, something that's never been done before. And I'd like all my fans and friends to come and see me."

So they did. And Dick walked out on stage, told a couple of jokes and he died. Literally. He dropped dead right on the stage. What a tragic end to a good man's life. I always wondered if Dick is sitting back somewhere getting a big kick out of the whole thing.

CHARLTON HESTON

Tom Leathers, the publisher of the Kansas City *Squire* for all those years, was a great friend. He passed away about three years ago. Tom wrote an article in *The Squire*, I think it was called "Can Mike Murphy Succeed in Talk Radio." A lot of people wrote in their opinions. Some said I couldn't do it. But I did. I fooled 'em.

People thought that a disc jockey who played records couldn't translate into talk radio. But they did and I think I was one of the first. And I ended up being in talk radio for twenty-five years. And that was after I'd been a disc jockey at KMBZ for ten years, so I was in talk radio two and a half times longer than I was a disc jockey.

But I think the highlight of the whole thing might've come the day I had Charlton Heston on. He was in town to do a movie about a mining expedition to find some gold that was buried somewhere.

Anyway, Charlton Heston came to the studio and they said, "Charlton Heston is waiting in the hall to meet you." Wow. So I walked up to him and said, "Hi, I'm Mike Murphy. You're going to be on my show with me." He said, "Great. Listen, do you happen to have a phone I can use?"

At that time I had a small office and I said, "Sure, c'mon in here. Have a seat at my desk, use the phone, you can have the whole thing."

So Charlton Heston sits down and puts his feet up on my desk and gets on the phone. And I thought, "My goodness. Here's Moses, and he's sitting at my desk with his feet up on it making a telephone call."

Well, he was just a great guy. When we got on the air he talked about all his movies. I remember asking him about the staff that Aaron had given him when he said, "Aaron, give me my staff." And he threw it down and it turned into a snake. He also used it to part the Red Sea. That was some powerful staff. So I asked him, "What ever became of that staff you used in the movie?" And he said, "You know, I have that in my office. It's right alongside my desk and I look at it every day."

We seemed to really hit it off and down through the years I'd give him a call every six months or so to see how he was doing. Sometimes I'd get him to do a phone interview on the show. Then he came back a couple of years ago and we had another great time. He was just really a great guy.

The last time he was on with me I'd sent him a bottle of whiskey, something like Drambuie or Courvoisier. Yeah, it was Courvoisier, which was brandy. He wrote me back the nicest letter and said, "You know, after doing your show, that bottle of brandy was the most enjoyable part of the trip. I just want to thank you for that and for your company." What a great man. Sadly, he just passed away earlier this year.

.

Mike and Mayor Charles Wheeler

Mike on Warpaint

Walter Cronkite

KCMO crew – Dave Dawson, Marshall
Saper, Bill Waris, Conrad Dobler, Mike

Cattle drive "just before the stampede"

At KC Masterpiece Barbecue: Mike,
George Brett, and others at the
"Salvation Army Show"

Mike's kids Pat, Susan, and Jenny

Loch Ness—Mike and the doctor
from London

Margaret Tynan, mayor of Kilkenny, Peter Farrelly, town clerk,
Billy Brett, Kilkenny Chamber of Commerce, Joe Stapleton,
town sergeant, Jack Walsh, marketing officer, South East Tour-
ism, John Kerry Keane, editor, *Kilkenny People*. Kneeling:
Sir Michael Murphy, KMBZ Kansas City.

Commemorative stone of the St. Patrick's
Day Parade at Italian Gardens

St. Patrick's Day Parade

St. Patrick's Day Parade

World Contact Day: Mike, Dan Hogerty, Mother Merz

Victor the Bear at the opening of Wycliff
West apartments

Cathy and Mike

The Gladstone is brought back from
Kilkenny

St. Patrick's Parade is born (1972)

KMBZ Odd Squad I.D. card

The Liberation of Paola, Kansas

Mike and Pat Murphy –
Ottumwa Day at the Royals

Tiny Tim and Mike

Mike and his lifetime friend Dan Hogerty

Tige Andrews—the head of *The Mod Squad* meets the Odd Squad

Steve Allen tells Mike a good one!

Mike and Monsignor Tighe before parade

The tiny plane Dan Hogerty had to board to go to Loch
Ness in Scotland

Mike in Dublin's Russell Court Hotel with Jimmy and Bridgett and Mary. Background is painting of Gladstone, the man.

Mike and the man from Bass Weejuns

Mayor Richard Berkley, Pearl Bailey,
and Mike

Mike and Richard Harris

Mike on the banks of Loch Ness,
in front of Urquhart Castle

Mike and Minnesota Fats

With Kansas City's own Marilyn Maye—guest
seventy-six times on *The Tonight Show*
(Johnny Carson). Mike had her on more.

Charlton Heston and Mike

Cy Perkins at the first St. Patrick's Day.
"Where the hell is everybody?"

Walt Lochman and Mike at the Mike
Murphy "jog-in"

Mike and Miss Paola after the Liberation.

Fifty parades ended at Kelly's. "Oh, my God,
what have I done?"

CLOSE ENCOUNTERS OF THE WEIRD KIND

From my earliest days I've always had this fascination with the un-known – UFOs, aliens, crop circles, conspiracy theories, mysteries.

The day of my last show in Kansas City, December 17, 2004, at Kelly's Westport Inn – an amazing story by itself which I'll address in more detail after the children are in bed –I told the crowd the story of what happened to my daughter and my wife one night while I was asleep.

When I started going with Cathy, I was sixteen and I told her that I thought I was an alien. This was pretty weird and of course she and her mother thought I was just totally crazy. (*You probably do too, by now.*) So all through the years, my wife's kind of wondered about me and my pre-occupation with aliens and UFOs. I told her, "One day they're gonna come and take me back where I came from."

So about 1979 I was doing the morning show on KCMO from 5 a.m. to 9 a.m. I had to get up about 3 a.m. to get to the station by 5 a.m., so I almost always went to bed early. Well, about ten o'clock one night I was in bed fast asleep. The next morning when I got home from work my wife told me that last night our daughter, Susan, said, "Mom, there's something in the backyard. Let's go look at it." So they walked out the back onto the deck, and there above the trees was a beautiful, golden, perfectly dome-shaped flying saucer with beams of light in the windows. It was about fifty feet above the ground, not thirty yards from the house. It was kind of swaying up and down, and through its windows they could see shadows of beings walking back and forth. They were that close. Susan, said, "Mom. Can they see us? Do they know we're watching them?" And it stayed there for ten or fifteen minutes…just hovered there, and then it left.

When they told me about it, I said, "See? I've been telling you that since I was a kid. I knew one day they were gonna come for me." And from that day on, my wife has never been the same. It really had a profound effect on her and on Susan.

I never really learned exactly what went on that night until that last show at Kelly's. It turns out what they think really happened was they were victims of one of these "abductions" people talk about — taken aboard the ship. Our daughter has been "regressed" by hypnosis since then and she talks about it. She says that that night they came down the hall in our house and shined a light in on me while I was asleep, that they were, in effect, looking for me. I never really heard the details all those years because I guess maybe I didn't want to hear it, I didn't want to know what was going on. But it was really a great adventure for them and I wish I'd have been part of it. Here I was, all my life talking about UFOs and aliens, drawing pictures when I was a kid, having UFO experts as guests on my show, and I'd never really seen one myself. At least, not that I remember.

SUSAN'S STORY

From Mike's daughter, Susan:

This is a "getting ready to go back to school story." It was around 1979 and I was getting ready to go to bed. School had just started back up and I was heading into my sophomore year in high school. But I wasn't in the routine of getting things organized for school yet. I was watching the ten o'clock news with Mom. (Dad was already in bed because he had to get up early for his morning show.) And Mom looks out the windows of the sliding glass doors of our old house at 103rd and Lee Boulevard. She says, "What is that?" So we both get up, open the doors, and go out onto the deck. And we see this rectangle kind of harvest-moon gold color coming toward us... and we're staring at it and it's coming at us from the east... and it comes to the treetops in our backyard, which was about a half-acre. Then it stops and rotates around 360 degrees and when it comes out it's just like a cartoon picture of a UFO. You could see the windows as it starts hovering over the trees... and it's enormous... maybe as big as half a football stadium. And we just stand there staring at it and it's not making a sound. We just stood there not talking for about forty-five seconds and then I said to Mom, "Do you think it knows we're watching it?" Mom says, "I don't know, but if it gets any closer, we're going inside."

And with that, it kind of took off to the north. We went back inside and we were both in kind of a daze. So Mom called to neighbors up the street to see if they saw it, but they didn't. So we went back and woke Dad up and told him what had happened and he said, "If it was a UFO, it came to see me." Dad had done hundreds of shows about UFOs and aliens and other paranormal things. It was funny, though. None of us talked about it much for five years or so. But that was the beginning of UFOs coming into Mike Murphy's backyard.

COMIC RELIEF

I went to the doctor today and he said, "I've got some bad news and some worse news." I said, "What's the bad news?" He says, "You've only got one day to live." I said, "My God, what's the worse news?" He says, "I should have told you yesterday."

In most books like this, people tell you how poor they were when they were younger. But I'm not going to tell you anything like that. When I was growing up, we were ALL poor. The reason I know this is because nobody ever had any money.

CHUCK YEAGER

It's hard to say who my best guest was or who my worst guest was, but one of the most unusual was a guy named Chuck Yeager, maybe the greatest test pilot that ever lived. He was the first person to break the sound barrier in 1947.

Remember the movie *The Right Stuff*? Some military people tend to be a little different. So we got him booked on the show and all the TV stations showed up with their remote trucks. I meet Chuck Yeager and walk into this room where he looks out the window and says, "What's all that?" And I said, "Oh, that's just the TV station's trucks."

He walked out and told all the TV people, in no uncertain terms, to get their gear and their asses out of there or he wasn't gonna do the show. Well, they all left and he comes back and I'm thinking, "What am I gonna do with this guy?"

I said, "What was all that about?" He said, "Oh, those TV guys follow me all over the place. I said I'd do your show, but I don't want them around." So we sat and had a nice visit. I asked him, "I heard you have 20-10 vision. What's that?" He said, "Whattaya mean what is that? You know what that is?" I said, "No, that's why I asked." He said, "It means

I have perfect vision. It means I can see an eagle sitting in a tree from five miles away. It means I can shoot a deer from six hundred yards away without a scope." Chuck Yeager. One very odd guy indeed.

BURL IVES

I had Burl Ives on the show one day. He was a great folk singer and actor. He had the hit song "A Little Bitty Tear," and around Christmastime you can always hear him singing, "Have a holly, jolly Christmas…"

In his acting career, he's probably best remembered for his role as Big Daddy in *Cat on a Hot Tin Roof* with Paul Newman and Elizabeth Taylor. He got an Academy Award and a lot of people thought he got it for that, but actually it was for a movie named *Big Country* with Gregory Peck and Jean Simmons that came out the same year. He was named Best Supporting Actor.

He came to town one time and he was scheduled to be on the show. That morning, when he hadn't shown, I called his hotel room and said, "Hi, Burl, this is Mike Murphy, you're supposed to be on my show this morning." He said, "Yeah, I know it. But you know, I'm lying here in bed with Momma and it's warm in here and it's cold outside. And I just thought, 'Maybe I'll just stay here.'" I said, "Burl, that sounds like a great idea. You just do that and maybe we'll get together next time around."

Then, as an afterthought, I said, "By the way, Burl, you won an Oscar for that movie, *Big Country*. I always wonder what people do with those statues, where they display them." He said, "You know, quite truthfully,

I use it as a doorstop. Don't really give a damn about the thing." Burl Ives, great man, great talent. Carl Sandburg once called him "the mightiest ballad singer born in any century."

WILLIAM SHATNER

One of the most fun times I ever had, I was doing the show from Los Angeles for a week and one of the guests we had scheduled was William Shatner. Shatner has become so big, he does those Priceline.com commercials and he stars on the wonderful TV show, *Boston Legal*, with James Spader and Candice Bergen, one of the best shows ever.

His career has been so good. Of course he started on the original *Star Trek* as Captain James T. Kirk of the *Starship Enterprise*. Then he went on to become police Sergeant T.J. Hooker on the show of the same name. Whatever he does he seems to do well. He's had a great career for a long time.

He was coming on the show to plug the latest *Star Trek* movie, I forget which one. We were doing the show from KISS in Los Angeles, and when it came time for Shatner to be there, Shatner wasn't there. It was about 9:15 a.m. and he was supposed to be there at 9:00. I'm thinking, "What am I gonna do? I got an hour to kill and nothing to talk about. No Shatner, no nothing."

So right about then, somebody said in my ear piece, "Mr. Shatner has entered the building." So here comes Shatner running down the hall, and he comes in the studio and says, "Sorry I'm late. The guard wouldn't let me in the building." I said, "Whattaya mean?" He said, "Well, I've got my dog and I've got my truck and we park and I'm bringing my dog in with me. My dog goes wherever I go. So the guard tells me, 'You're not coming in here with that dog!' And I say, 'Look, you know who I am? I'm Captain Kirk from the *Starship Enterprise*.' And the guard says, 'Look, I don't know who you are, I never heard of you, but you're not bringing that dog in here!'"

So he said, "I had to go back to the car, put the dog inside, crack the window, lock the door, and run back to the studio. I'm sorry I'm late." So we went on to have a great visit. He's just a regular guy, real likable and funny. It turns out that he's a horseman and he comes to Kansas City every year for the American Royal. He wears a ball hat and sunglasses and nobody even knows he's here. He doesn't want to make a big deal of himself. What was interesting was that in a recent episode of *Boston Legal* he had a fling with a woman rancher who had horses and it showed them riding along together and I wondered if that was his way of working his love for horses into the show.

Back to the interview, at one point I asked him, "Look, with all the shows and movies you've made about space travel and extraterrestrial life, have you ever seen a flying saucer?" He said, "You know, I have a big interest in that stuff. I'll tell you this. One night I was riding my motorcycle and I was out in the desert. I got off my bike and I'm looking at the stars. Then, on a whim, I said out loud, 'You know, if you creatures are really out there, I'd think you'd want to talk to me a little bit.'" He said, "About that time what I saw up in the sky just made me crazy." I said, "What was it?" He said, "Well, it was a light. It just hovered there for a few seconds, then whoosh, it was gone." I said, "What do you think?" He said, "I believe in 'em. I believe." That was William Shatner, one of my all-time favorite interviews.

Before Shatner left the studio I looked out the window, and across the street there was a Denny's Restaurant, and just to the right of it there was some construction going on and there was this enormous crane.

This thought hit me and I said to him, "You know, I just got an idea. If you ever do another TV series, why don't you call yourself Denny Crane!" Imagine that.

MARSHALL SAPER

When I decided to get back into the radio business after being out a year, a man named Mike McGee came to me and he said, "KCMO has always been kind of a 'do nothing' station. They've got a great signal, but they've never done much with ratings in this town. So now we're gonna take it and we're gonna make it a talk station. And we'd like you to come and be on it." A guy named Steve Shann said, "Let's get you to sign a contract." So we went out to my joint, the Pizza Paddle, and signed it over a pitcher of beer on some beer-stained napkins that Steve had written it on. That was in 1980.

So they had hired Marshall Saper and they said, "He's gonna do a show about brains and psychology and you're gonna do a show about cannibals and zombies." And Marshall and I became good friends. He'd have us out to his house and we'd get together. He was just terrific at what he did and everybody loved him.

I'll never forget the day when it was all over for Marshall, when he took his own life, or so they say he did. My nephew, "FS Meatsauce," called and said, "Have you heard the news?" I think it was on a Sunday morning, maybe November – it was cold. And he said, "They say Marshall Saper has killed himself." And I said, "Oh, no. Not Marshall."

But the story was that Marshall had killed himself because of some sort of scandal that was going to come out about him and a female patient that he was allegedly involved with. I don't know how much of that was true, but a lot of people around town started thinking that the circumstances were pretty fishy.

Here are some of the facts: They found him in the parking lot of Humana Hospital. Now, why would a man who wanted to kill himself be found near an emergency room? The weirdest thing was that he was shot twice, in the chest or stomach. They say nobody trying to commit suicide with a gun would ever shoot themselves in the stomach. And TWICE? People were also suspicious of a suicide note that was typewritten, another unlikely scenario.

People called in with all kinds of theories. Some said he'd been critical of the fancy, expensive rehab country clubs around town and that ruffled some feathers. Those kinds of things always pop up after something like this happens.

All I know is that Marshall Saper was a good man and a good friend and he's been greatly missed, by the city and myself.

SISTERS

At the old St. Mary's School in Ottumwa, one of the nuns was Sister Dolores. And in my early grades, before she was a nun, she dressed in street clothes and she was just beautiful! She was a "postulant," that's the word, which is a candidate to join a religious order, before they take their final vows.

She was gorgeous. She was about twenty-two years old. And by the time I got to fourth grade, she was a full-fledged nun in the long habit and all of that. But I always had quite a schoolboy crush on her and she liked me a lot, and we'd follow each other around and talk and joke.

And I always kept track of her. I heard she'd left the church to marry a man who had been a priest and had also left the church. So one day, years later, I decided to track her down and surprise her by telling her it was her old student, Mike Murphy.

Well, I got her phone number and called her up and said, "Sister Dolores? It's me, Mike Murphy from Saint Mary's in Ottumwa." And she said, "Who?" And I said, "Mike Murphy. You used to be my favorite teacher." Then she said, "No. I'm sorry, but I don't remember you. I remember someone else in your class, but I don't remember you."

Boy. Talk about having someone burst your balloon. I was floored. It just goes to show, you never know who's gonna remember you and who isn't. As my friend, Walt Coffey, likes to say, "Thirty years from now nobody will ever know we were alive." But who knows, this book may be sitting in somebody's library collecting dust.

In seventh grade, Sister Rosemary and I hit it off like thieves. I always got the feeling that she liked me a little too much. But she was just beautiful and she really liked me. I don't know what it was with nuns and me. Maybe they liked the fact that I was pretty funny and a little irreverent.

So I looked up Sister Rosemary and called the nunnery where she was and asked for her. They said, "I'm sorry, Sister Rosemary has dementia." Wow. Another blast of the cold winds of reality! "Gather your rosebuds while ye may" has always been excellent advice.

Another was Sister Mathias. In high school she said, "Mike, you're a great actor. I want you to do drama and all these things." So I got into doing dramatic readings in speech class and ended up winning the state contest for some dramatic readings I did. The finals were in Storm Lake, Iowa. I won for a reading I did called "Afraid of the Dark."

Sister Mathias was really excited for me and she said, "Mike, now I'm gonna have you do a play. We're gonna do *Home of the Brave*." I remember all the seniors were mad because I was just a junior and I got the lead. But Sister Mathias getting me into speech, prepared me for what I wound up doing.

I fell in love with Storm Lake, Iowa. I told my wife, Cathy, "That's where we're going on our honeymoon." Dick van Dyke did a movie there called *Cold Turkey*. It was the neatest little city I'd ever seen. So when Cathy and I got back there, the lake had dried up. So there we were in Storm Lake and there was no lake. I'm sure they probably still have storms once in a while.

THE LIBERATION OF PAOLA, KANSAS

It was about 1968 and I'd been in the radio business for about ten years. My son, Patrick, was in first grade and we'd moved three times in the past year to go to different radio jobs. So when we got to Kansas City, Patrick said, "Dad, can we just stay here?" And I thought, maybe that's a good idea.

I started working the night shift, from 9 p.m. to 12 midnight, at KMBZ. And it was like I was a bullet that'd been shot out of a gun. I knew I was pretty good, but I wanted to be successful, so I worked really hard on my new show. People started calling the station manager, Walt Lochman, and saying, "You oughtta put Murphy on in the morning."

So in December that year, they did. And things really took off fast. This town loved me and I loved this town. Everything I did, the town took to, and everything the town did, I took to. It was a perfect relationship.

About that time a story hit the newspapers about Paola, Kansas, and I thought that was pretty funny because in the radio business there was this big scandal going on called "Payola." They said that Alan Freed and Dick Clark and others had been taking money under the table from record companies to play the current records they were promoting. In those days

I used to play whatever records I wanted. There were no play lists or set up programs from marketing wizards.

So this Payola scandal was going on about the same time I heard of Paola, Kansas, so I went down there one day and I thought, "There's gotta be a way I can do this and make some fun out of it." So I figured out that all the people who lived in Paola lived there because they were "captives" and they couldn't get out.

There was barbed wire or something keeping them all there. If they could've left, they would've, but they couldn't because they were being held against their wills.

So I went on the air and said, "We're gonna liberate the town of Paola, Kansas, and I will be their liberator." And at that time, whatever I said people would want to get in on.

So I said, "We'll meet at Metcalf South on Saturday morning," and I said, "Bring all your weapons, water pistols, etc." We had some bunnies from the Playboy Club with us. A buddy of mine named Billy Whipple brought a submarine on a flatbed truck. It had big guns and it looked like we were going to war.

So people started massing and there must have been ten thousand of us "liberators." They formed a line from Metcalf South almost all the way back to the city. It must've been ten miles long. As we moved to Paola and poured into that town, it was like D-Day and the people on the street were shooting marshmallows out of slingshots. So it turned into one big party, everybody having a great time.

So from that day on I became known as the Great Liberator of Paola, Kansas.

EWING KAUFFMAN

When I first came to Kansas City in 1968, one of the first people I heard about was Ewing Kauffman, a local legend and founder of Marion Labs, who was in the process of buying the Kansas City Royals. I wanted to meet Ewing, and I found out he was a member of the very ritzy Kansas City Club downtown at 9th and Baltimore. Well I thought it'd be a good idea to go down there and say hello to him and maybe play pool with him. (When I lived in Ottumwa, Iowa, all we did, me and my brother, Pat, was play pool, so we got pretty good at it.)

I had heard rumors that some days Ewing would lose $15,000 or $20,000 during lunch playing pool down there. That sounded like a pretty good opportunity for a young, struggling disc jockey. But the problem was, you had to be a member of the Kansas City Club to get in, play pool, eat, do anything.

Well luckily I had a great friend – best friend I ever had – named Pat O'Neill and I went to Pat and I said, "Pat, is there any way I can get into this Kansas City Club?" And you know he said, "My mother, Maggie, is on the board of the club and I'll present it to her and we'll see if we can get you in." So they did. And this other friend of mine, a guy named Bill

Morse, was also on the board. So the two of them voted for me and I guess I must have gotten a couple of other votes, because this poor transplant from Iowa got in!

So now I'm a member of the Kansas City Club. This is as elite as it gets in this town. They still had a "Women Not Allowed" policy. Well, they were allowed, but only on the upper floor, the top floor where they had dancing and such. But the Oak Room downstairs, where the pool tables were, was men only and I was figuring, if I could just find Mr. Kauffman and get him to play a game of pool, I might win $15,000 or $20,000, which was as much as I made in a year! Sadly, that never happened.

But I did get to know Ewing and he was a great, great man. Whenever I was in a restaurant with anybody and he walked in the door, he'd say, "I'm picking up the tab for the whole place!" What a person. Kansas Citians were truly lucky to have a man like Ewing Kauffman be a part of their town.

.

MY ST. LOUIS BLUES

The year was 1985. The Kansas City Royals were playing the St. Louis Cardinals. Both teams from Missouri. They called it the "Show Me Series," and "The I-70 Series." It was an exciting series, a lot of back and forth, it went to seven games, and the Royals won.

In the course of these human events, a disc jockey named Ron Morgan, at KMOX, St. Louis, would start coming on my show and I started going on his. We made a bet that whichever team lost, that we'd have to move to the other guy's city and do the show for a week.

Well, I knew I didn't want to go to St. Louis so I was praying for the Royals to win... and they did! So Ron had to come here and do my show for a week. We had a great time, he's a great guy. And during that week, the man who ran KMOX was listening to the shows and he got to thinking I was pretty good. So not too long after that, he called me and said, "How'd you like to come to work at KMOX?" I said, "Oh, my goodness, I don't know." I had some pretty strong roots in Kansas City by now. He said, "Well, let me get with my people and we'll write you up an offer."

Well, they sent me an offer and the money was huge! And everybody was telling me, "You've gotta go to KMOX." Their longtime morning guy,

Jack Carney, had recently died. He had started there with WIL back in the 1950s, then moved to San Francisco to KSFO (the station I always wanted to go to), where he was "Mr. San Francisco," then he came back to KMOX and became a hero and had high ratings. KMOX is one of the greatest radio stations in the country and had been for years. I used to listen to it when I started out in the business. I was just down the road in Springfield and I'd pick up their signal with no trouble. I'd hear "the man that walks and talks at midnight," John McCormick and all the great staff, Jim White and Bob Hardy, and then, of course, Cardinal baseball with Harry Caray and Jack Buck.

Anyway, the offer came and I didn't want to go. But I told them I'd come and start the first of the year in 1986. But as the time to move got closer, I went back to my boss at KCMO and said, "Listen, I've been thinking it over and I really don't want to go to St. Louis." He said, "Well, you've already quit and I can't bring you back now at the money you were making so you gotta go."

So that was the name of that song. "Off we go to St. Louis." I was nervous because I knew it was risky to follow a local legend like Jack Carney, no matter who you are. And I was right to be nervous, it turned into a nightmare.

Right from the getgo, the station manager, Bob Hyland, and I didn't hit it off. He wanted people to call him "God." He would have meetings in his office at 7:30 in the morning, just the time the sun would be coming up behind the arch, and he would frame himself in the arch with the sun behind him.

And he told people, "You may refer to me as God."

He'd call me into his office from time to time and say, "Look, this is a pile of mail from people who don't like you and I want you to read it." One day he did it and that got me. I went over to his desk, picked up the letters, tore them up and threw 'em in his wastebasket. It wasn't long after that, they called and said, "Meet us out at Busch Gardens." Hyland sent some of his henchmen and they said, "You're done." And that was that.

But for the record, when I came, the great Jack Carney's share of market ratings was 12 or 13, and I had gotten 'em up to a 19! I was in the newspapers every day with people asking, "How can you do this? How can you replace the great Jack Carney?" I thought to myself, "Hell, Hyland says he's God, maybe he can get Carney back!"

But St. Louis is a great radio town and it has great people. I'd be walking along the street and a bus'd go by and someone would stick his head out and yell, "Hey, Murphy!" Really a nice bunch of people. I really enjoyed the times I had outside the station. My old buddy Art Fleming was there.

The first night we were in town, in a hotel down by the river, the phone rings and Cathy answers it and says, "Jack's on the line for you." I said, "Jack? Jack who?" She said, "Jack Buck." I said, "He's calling me?" She said, "Yeah, c'mon."

So I get on the phone and I hear (gravelly voice), "This is Jack Buck. There's a house down the street for sale and I thought you might want to take a look at it." Just the nicest guy in the world. When I started working he said, "What kind of a guy is Hank Stram?" (The Chief's coach from the Super Bowl years.) I said, "He's a good guy." They were both working on Monday Night Football back then. Jack said, "Well, he steals my candy bars. I always bring a candy bar and Hank will steal it." I said, "Here's what you do: You get yourself a piece of steel, coat it with chocolate, and let him bite into that!" Jack said, "That's a terrific idea!"

Jack said, "It's gonna be fun working with you. But I don't want to do that morning show. When they have a vacancy in the nine o'clock to noon spot, they always call me. so listen, don't you get fired!" So when I did get fired, he looked at me with tears in his eyes and said, "I told you not to do this!"

It was one of the best shows I ever had, but there're a lot of people in that city, and while their ratings were up, the stacks of mail were what counted to them. Weird.

VICTOR THE BEAR

When I came to Kansas City I would do almost anything. And I did most everything. I had some great friends, and when those friends asked me to do something, I'd do it. One of the best friends I ever had was a man named Cy Perkins. He managed an apartment project in Kansas City called Wycliff West.

At that time – about the early seventies – the saying was, "There's nothing west of Wycliff." Of course today, there's a lot west of Wycliff. And a lot south of Wycliff. Hell, for ten miles in any direction, all you can see are houses and apartments and shopping malls and strip centers and churches and schools.

It proves a whole lotta people must think Kansas City is a great place to live. And it is!

So one day Cy said, "We're doing an advertising promotion to get people interested in Wycliff West. We're gonna bring in this bear that wrestles people and I wonder if you'd come down and wrestle the bear." Well, in the paper the next day, they had a story that the bear had come to town and wrestled the mayor, who at that time was Dr. Charles Wheeler, one of my greatest friends and one of Kansas City's greatest mayors.

So I thought, "Well, if the mayor can do it, I can probably do it, too." So I got there on a Saturday morning and there's Victor the Bear and they told me, "There's gonna be nothing to this. This bear does this all the time. It'll be like dancing with your sister. All you have to do is get up there and stand and the bear will give you a gentle hug and that'll be it." Now they said it was an "Alaskan brown bear." (I found out later that an Alaskan brown bear and a grizzly bear are the same species.) So this bear in front of me was eight feet tall, weighed a thousand pounds, and I'm supposed to pick a fight with it.

The bear has gloves on over the claws and a muzzle on its face, but when I looked into its eyes, it looked right back into mine and I could swear this bear took an instant dislike to me. So anyway, I stand up and the bear grabs hold of me and starts to squeeze and it was like every bone in my spine cracked at once. It made a loud crunch, kind of like when you used to open those old metal ice trays. But louder. I said, "My back's been broken." So the trainer comes up and finally gets the bear and me apart. He says, "Are you all right?" I said, "I think so." I knew I was still alive. Then he tells me, "Stand here and we'll get a picture taken with you and the bear." I was a little nervous but I said okay. So the bear sits down and crosses his legs, sitting there like a big, hairy man and I'm sitting just to the right of him. Suddenly the bear hauls off and hits me smack in the mouth! My nose starts bleeding. My jaw feels funny. So here I am: my back's broken, my nose is bleeding, my jaw may be dislocated… and Victor the Bear is just sitting there and I look through his muzzle and suddenly I know he's thinking, "I got you real good, buddy." I never thought I'd see a grizzly bear smile, but that day it sure looked that way.

LIBERACE AND MOUNTAIN SHADOWS

Well, I knew Cy Perkins felt real bad about the incident with Victor the Bear. His trainer had told Cy he'd never seen Victor act that way with anyone else before. Well, we were even because I'd never had a bear act that way with me before. Or since.

But anyway, a little while after that, as payback for the Victor the Bear fight, Cy says, "You ever been to Phoenix?" I said, "No." He said, "I'm gonna take you to Mountain Shadows, you and your wife and me and my wife and we'll have a great time in Phoenix." So we all went to Mountain Shadows in Phoenix and we had one of the best times in our lives. And that's where I made all my Phoenix connections, with the racetrack and Dan Hogerty and all that.

So when we get there Cy says, "I'm gonna take you to a restaurant tonight called Etienne's" -- a French restaurant, where we had the best meal we'd ever eaten. And while we were there, a man came in and sat behind us. I took a look at him and I said to my wife, "That's Liberace." And it was! So after we finished our meal I went over and said, "You're Liberace." Well, he gave me that great big smile of his and said, "Yes, I am. Why don't you come over here and sit down for a minute?" He was sitting with his brother, George. On his TV show back in the fifties, I remember how he'd always say, "And this is my brother, George." People would love that part. So after I sat down, Liberace brought his hand up and said, "Look at these." And he showed me all the rings he had on his fingers and told me about them. And we had a nice long chat and that more than made up for the whole Victor the Bear episode. If I have to choose between Victor the Bear and Liberace, I'll pick Liberace any day!

JIM FOWLER

One of my favorite shows of all time was *Mutual of Omaha's Wild Kingdom*. It'd be on every Sunday night and people just loved it. The host was Marlon Perkins and he'd go all over the world to find animals in the wild. His sidekick was named Jim Fowler.

It was a funny relationship they had. Marlon would say things like, "While Jim tries to milk the enraged rhinoceros, I'll have a martini here in this tree." Can you imagine milking a rhinoceros, who was not only just a rhinoceros, but was enraged?

Now that's mean. It seemed like Marlon got most of the glory and Jim got most of the dangerous assignments.

One day Jim Fowler came on the show. I thought, "Boy, this is neat. What a great guy and what great stories he must have to tell." Jim said to me, "I made a movie with Sigourney Weaver called *Gorillas in the Mist*." Sigourney Weaver is a gorgeous woman and a terrific actress.

Jim said, "I was the animal consultant and I wanted to do a good job and have her like me. So I started running up and down the mountain and I screwed up my knee. The doctor said I had to have a knee replacement and he told me I was in luck because a gorilla had just died and we could perform the first gorilla-to-human knee replacement. It would work, but there were side effects."

The side effects were, they told him, when he woke up in the morning, he'd want to beat his chest. He'd want to live in a tree, and he'd have to eat fifty bananas a day.

"The doctor was pretty excited about it and he said to think about what a great scientific achievement that would be. So I thought about it overnight and I told them I really didn't want to do it. They said, 'That's too bad. Just think how fast you could run!' Ha-ha."

But Jim was a great guest and he used to come here and be on the show with me every year or so. He was one of the most popular guests and he told great stories. He was always jumping out of planes and lassoing wild buffalo and wrestling with monkeys. So I asked him one time what was the scariest thing that'd happened to him. He said, "Probably one of the scariest – and most famous - was the one where Marlon had me down in the South American jungle and he wanted me to go in the water with a giant snake – a boa constrictor of some kind.

"Well, I get in the water with it and it decided right away that it was gonna eat me. He managed to get his body coiled around mine a couple of times and got my arm in its mouth up to the shoulder. And I'm thinking all the time, '*Don't panic.*' And I'm wondering, 'What does that mean, Don't panic? People have their heads in grizzly bears' mouths or a rogue elephant is charging them and they tell 'em, '*Don't panic.*'

"So I just stayed as calm as I could and Marlon is over there on the banks of the river drinking his martini. And I'm wondering what the heck I'm gonna do. Finally we got some help from somewhere and we were able to pull the snake off of me. But that was certainly the scariest time I ever had."

What a great guest and what a great guy.

MINNESOTA FATS AND ROGER THE PLUMBER

I mentioned shooting pool and Ewing Kauffman and playing at the Kansas City Club. Knowing that I was a pool shooter, Bill Morse, then lieutenant governor of Missouri, called me one day and said, "How'd you like to meet Minnesota Fats?"

The Minnesota Fats! *The Hustler*, with George C. Scott, Paul Newman, and Jackie Gleason was one of my all-time favorite movies. So I said, "Great!" And he said, "Well, we've gotta go to St. Louis." I said, "Let's go!" So Bill sent a police car to my house to pick me up and take me to the Municipal Airport, which has since been named Wheeler Downtown Airport after our marvelous, legendary mayor, Charles B.

So Bill and I got on a plane and flew to St. Louis. At that time Minnesota Fats was starring in a movie called *The Player*. It was kinda like *The Hustler* but not nearly as good. But I got to meet Minnesota Fats and I said, "If you're ever in Kansas City I'd like to see you."

Well, sure enough, he comes to Kansas City and we go out to shoot some pool. We went down to the Muhlebach Hotel (I had called ahead) and they'd set up a pool table out in their lobby. So it was me and my brother, Pat, who could just shoot the eyes outta the balls. I said, "Fats, we'll play you a game." Fats said, "All right, I'll play ya!" We decided to play Straight Pool ("Call Your Shot"), which is the same game they played in *The Hustler*. Well, for openers, my brother ran 45 balls! Then Minnesota Fats got to shoot and he miscued. Then I shot and ran about 23 balls. Then my brother shot another 25 or 30. We're up to about 75 now and Minnesota Fats doesn't have anything. And I shoot and I get 20 or 30 and I'm up over 50. Then Minnesota Fats got another tough leave and miscued again. He threw the cue on the floor and said, "I quit!" So he didn't make a ball, but Pat and I did get our picture taken with him.

Well, I had that picture of me, my brother, and Minnesota Fats hanging by the stairs going down to the basement of my house. And my friend who was often on my show, Roger the Plumber, comes over to fix our water heater one day. He says, "You need a new one. It's probably gonna run about $500." So I said okay and he puts it in and when he's done he says, "I can see you've got a pool table." I said, "Sure." He said, "You wanna shoot?" And I said, "Oh, I don't play much anymore." He said, "I'll tell you what. I'll play you for the water heater." I said, "Well, sure, I guess so. I'll tell you what, let's play for the water heater and another $400." He said, "Yeah, that'll be okay!" So within half an hour I had won a $500 water heater and an extra $400 in cash. And as Roger and I are going upstairs, he sees the picture of me, my brother, and Minnesota Fats with our pool cues on the wall and he looks at that and says, "I'll be damned! I wish I'd have seen that picture on the way down!"

FS MEATSAUCE

I'm Greg Schmidt, I'm Mike's nephew and good friend. My mom is Mike's sister. Mike calls me "FS Meatsauce." He gave me that name a long time ago, I'm not really sure why, but it is kinda funny.

I moved to Kansas City in the fall of 1973. Mike and I were always close, but became a lot closer after I got here. When I think back on all the years, the thing that might be most synonymous with Mike is the St. Patrick's Day Parade. I wasn't at the first one – the one with just a few people and a goat. But I did make the second one and it was a little more organized and a little bit longer, but nothing compared to what it became over the years.

I'll always remember that parade, though. Mike had said, "Come on down, you'll love it." And I did and we ended up in front of Dan Hogerty's Bar down at 12th and Baltimore. Dan was a wonderful old Irishman who was so close to Mike. He was there with all the characters Mike and he hung around with: Pat O'Neill, Jim Lynch, Cy Perkins, and all the gang from Hogerty's.

The really fun thing was that Hogerty's Bar wasn't big enough to hold all the people so we ended up out in the street with a great street party going on. I remember a couple of hours into it, Mike looked over to me and I was involved in building a human pyramid. I think I was on the bottom level, four or five guys. And we had three or four guys on top of us. And a couple of guys on top of them. Of course, it all ended horribly when everything crashed down to the street. So we laughed and drank and had a good time.

And that was the first of twenty-five straight St. Patrick's Day Parades I was in. Every year was different. Every year was a great time. One of the best was the year that the parade started at Loose Park, went down through the Plaza, and ended at Westport in front of Kelly's. They barricaded the streets and it was maybe the best street party this town's ever seen.

It was beautiful weather that day, about seventy-five degrees, and I had some friends who'd come into town. The friend from New Jersey, Paul Carbone, got lost, and we went looking for him and found out he'd put on a bartender's apron and had gotten behind the bar at I think the New Stanley and was handing out beers and not charging anybody.

Another year my friend Mark was in town and did a cartwheel and split the seam of his green tuxedo pants from crotch to knees. It turned out a lot of girls got around him and pinned him back together with safety pins.

I'll always remember riding on the green garbage truck, which became Mike's standard mode of parade transportation when the parades got larger. I remember my father came down for the parade and it was real cold and it started to sleet and my dad looked at me and said, "What in the world are we doing in the roof of a garbage truck?"

But it was all good. We went to the Italian Gardens like we did for so many years after the parade and had a wonderful time in there. Mike always had all the notables in Kansas City around him.

People who were famous and not so famous were his good friends, and it was an opportunity for us to meet mayors and entertainers and authors—all of that on that great day.

One year, in fact, instead of riding on the garbage truck, Mike had a limousine lined up. And so he invited me to ride with him on that. That was really neat, although about two thirds of the way through the parade the limousine broke down... So we ended up having to push the limousine to the side of the curb and sat there and watched the rest of the parade. Somehow that seemed appropriate for guys like us.

So anyway, those are some of my memories of St. Patrick's Day through the years...always a ton of fun. I think it's a day that will always be synonymous with Mike in this town, and hopefully everybody who reads this will feel they're a part of that day.

SUPERMAN

I grew up in the best time there was ever gonna be – in the forties and the fifties. And when I was a kid and going to St. Mary's School in Ottumwa, Iowa, I'd come home every day – this must've been second or third grade – and turn on the radio because we didn't have TV. My favorite shows were *Superman, The Great Gildersleeve, Fibber McGee and Molly, Amos 'n' Andy*, and great shows like that.

When I got home, *Superman* would be on and that's maybe what got me so interested in science fiction. Superman could get crippled by Kryptonite or stop a speeding locomotive with one hand. I still think it was the greatest science fiction story of all time. The man from another planet that came here with all these powers.

So in our neighborhood we used to tie towels around our necks and see who could jump off the highest building. I'll just bet you there were kids all over America doing the same exact thing. Well, I got to the point that one time I jumped off the roof of our house. It must've been twenty feet and it seemed a lot higher. But I landed okay and I think I had the record in our neighborhood.

Anyway, radio was always a big thing to me when I was a kid. And then radio changed and the old serials went off, probably because most people were watching TV. But then Top 40 Radio came on the scene, at least that's what we all called it, and there was this station in Des Moines that I still think is the best station there ever was. It was KIOA and they had a guy in the morning named Frosty Mitchell and the McKinnon brothers, Don and Doug. Don went on to Los Angeles, and Doug stayed there and worked the all-night spot.

Doug was the funniest guy I ever heard on radio and I still talk to him from time to time. He did things with "drop-ins" and "cut-ins" and sound effects. And I stole all that for my own show. Some random recorded voice would come in and say, "Hey, Don, what are you doing?" And I'd say, "My name isn't Don and how'd you get in here?" We did that a lot and it was really fun. And the station got so good playing the popular music at the time, like Johnny Cash and Elvis and all the new music hitting the scene. And that was the beginning of "Top 40 Radio."

So when I got out of college and came back to Ottumwa, I started to work at KLEE radio and stayed there for a year. They sold the station and it was bought by a man from Chicago named Bill O'Connor, who was a commercial announcer who did commercials for Budweiser like "Pick a pair of six packs. Buy Bud."

When he came in, he heard me and said, "I want you to go to one of our other stations in a bigger city." So I went on to one of the stations he had in Springfield, Illinois. It was a wonderful place. It was 1959 and we had record hops. It was one of the best years of my life. I met my buddies. We all lived together because we didn't have enough money to live alone. So me and Jerry Gahn and a fella called Rock Hudson all lived together in a little house. And Rock Hudson went on to bigger things. He called himself Rock Hudson because Bill O'Connor thought that'd be a good name for him. He didn't look anything like the actor. And Jerry Gahn – the first time I met him he said, "I'm a Jew, you know." And I said, "I'm a Catholic. We'll get along fine." Jews and Catholics always seemed to hit it off real good for some reason.

I went back to Ottumwa in 1960 and married my wife, Cathy, and we went back to Springfield and just had a terrific time. Jerry went on to Rockford, Illinois, and Rock went back to Chicago. But I still talk to those guys. Back in those days it was something special. We said, "We're radio folk." We just thought we were a cut above the rest. Of course, we weren't. We had a reunion a couple of years ago back in Springfield and it was really something.

DAVID OGDEN STIERS

I didn't want to do sections about bad guests – people that I knew would be bad or good, but I thought I'd do a couple stories about bad people and good people. And the worst, maybe the worst human being I ever met. I don't even know if I can say this or not, but I will, and I don't care.

The people from *MASH* for the most part were good. I didn't have some of them on, but Jamie Farr was just marvelous, and he and I got to be good friends. He's really a neat guy.

But I had that guy David Ogden Stiers come on, and he sat down in the studio and he put his headset on and we opened the show with the theme from *MASH*. What else would you do when you'd have one of the characters from *MASH* come in but play the theme from *MASH*?

So he took his headset off and threw it against the wall and started cussing and saying, "Damn you! Damn you!"

I said, "What's going on?"

And he said, "Don't you know what the lyrics to that song are, you dumb ass?"

And I said, "What do you mean?"

This was not on the air, this was off the air, because the theme was still playing.

And he said, "The words to that that song are 'Suicide is dangerous.' This is the worst thing that's ever been."

It comes time to fade the theme out and open the mike and I said to him, on the air, "Are you ready to go?"

And he said, "Yeah, I guess."

So I said to him, on the air, "Look. We don't have to do this. We can just quit."

And he thought for a minute and figured he had to plug his appearance at Starlight or whatever it was, and he said, "Yeah, I wanna do it."

So I said to myself, "Look. If I have to do this beginning with somebody like this I can do anything."

So I did it, we did it, it was over, and I got it done. I didn't know if I could do it, but I did, and that was David Ogden Stiers.

GREGORY PECK

Gregory Peck came to town and the producer told me he was booked for tomorrow's show. I was already nervous enough and now I have to interview Gregory Peck, Captain Ahab, Atticus Finch, a true living legend!

Gregory Peck gets into my studio, which was a small one, and sits down, and we had a great time. I asked him what his favorite movie was and of course it was *To Kill a Mockingbird*. He talked about that and then we started talking about *Moby Dick*. He said, "It took two years to film *Moby Dick*. I had to get on that mechanical whale and get tied down... I almost drowned on several occasions! It was one tough movie to make."

But we went on to have a great talk, and I almost forget I'm in the presence of this great actor. He's six foot three, snow white hair, dignified. When he got up to leave, I said, "It was great doing this. I guess you realized I was a little nervous about interviewing someone who's such a legend."

He smiled and said, "Aw, hell. We're all just people." What a great thing to hear from a man like that. I've always remembered it whenever I had any kind of "nervous" interview.

We're all just people.

DON HO

I want to talk about another real legend, Don Ho. Everybody whoever went to Hawaii remembers Don Ho, "Mr. Tiny Bubbles." He was so good. Dean Martin wished he was as good as Don Ho. And when we went to see him sing in Hawaii, he heard I was in the audience and that I was from Kansas City and he loved the Kansas City Chiefs. So he said to the manager, "See if Mike'll come back and see me after the show."

So we went back to his suite and there in his quarters were about a hundred people. They were all ages and sizes; most looked Hawaiian. On the bed sat Don Ho, and beside him on the bed was his checkbook. And one at a time these people would come up to him and say, my name is – some long Hawaiian name I couldn't pronounce – and he would write them a check. This went on for about an hour. Every one of these people got a check from Don Ho. Little kids, mothers, grandpas… they'd all sit down on the bed next to Don Ho and he'd write them each a check. I have no idea how many of his friends and relatives Don Ho supported, but it was one of the most touching and generous things I'd ever witnessed. God bless Don Ho.

LOCH NESS, HOGERTY, AND THE WATER WITCH

When Hogerty and Lillian and Cathy and I went to Scotland to look for the monster, we went to Edinburgh where we had to rent a plane to get up to a little town called Drumnadrochit, which is right on the banks of Loch Ness. The name of the plane was Logan Air. It was very small and the door was even smaller. Dan Hogerty was a pretty big guy.

So here we are five thousand miles away from home to look for the Loch Ness Monster, the whole purpose of this trip, and we can't get Dan through the door of the plane, which was not wide enough to accommodate the breadth of Hogerty's butt.

So I get behind him and the pilot gets behind him and it's like we're trying to force several bags of potatoes in there. We get him halfway through the door, but we just can't get him in. Now he's stuck. And the pilot said, "Look, if we can't get this guy in the plane, I'm gonna have to cancel the deal." And I'm thinking, the plans of this trip are gonna go down the sewer cause we can't get Hogerty into the plane.

So I said, "Let me give him one more push." And I got back about ten feet and got a running start and crashed right into his butt and popped him into the plane. So we got in this little plane and flew over what looked to me like Antarctica with snow all over the place. It was cold. But we flew to Loch Ness and we got on the ground, rented a car, and drove to Drumnadrochit to a hotel that had no central heating. They said we'll have an old lady come to your room at ten o'clock and bring you a hot water bottle that you can put in bed with you.

The hot water bottle didn't stay hot very long and in the morning I said to Hogerty, "I've never been this cold in my life. We've gotta get outta here!" And Dan said, "Well, whatever you want to do." We found a hotel down the street that did have central heat, but that was a rare exception in those days. Call it a little Irish luck on the freezing plains of Scotland. And that was just the start of the adventure.

One night in the Drumnadrochit Hotel I met this doctor from London who took me in his boat out on the Loch Ness, figuring we were bound to see old Nessie. Well, we didn't see anything, but afterward he said to me, "Have you ever heard of Wing Commander Kerry?" I said no, and he said, "He was one of the most famous British pilots during World War II. I want to take you to meet him." I said, "Great," and he said, "Oh, by the way, his wife is 'Winnie the Witch.' Her name is Winifred Kerry and she's featured on all the Loch Ness Monster shows you see on television."

So we went to the house where they live, Wing Commander Kerry and Winnie Kerry, the Water Witch. We had a great visit with him about World War II. Then Winnie told me that all summer long flying saucers fly over Loch Ness, that they'd been doing that for years. The wing commander said, "Yeah, I don't know how they fly, but they go about ten thousand miles a second."

Anyway, Winnie got out her map of the Loch, and because she was a "water witch," she could tell where the monster was at any particular time. She said, "Let me see," and she took a pencil and said, "It's over here right now. Actually there are many of them."

Then I said, "Tell me about when you were a kid. How many times did you see them?" She said, "Oh, many times." I said, "When did you see one the first time?" She said, "I was a little girl." I said, "How big was it?" She got this wide look in her eyes and said, "Why, it was *colossal*!"

That was Wing Commander Kerry and his wife, Winnie, the Water Witch. What a great couple.

EVEL KNIEVEL AND FLYING SAUCERS

You know, as you get older, time seems to be going faster and faster. It's like you're a little kid riding on a sled. You start out going real slow down this easy hill, but as you get into your twenties and thirties the hill starts to get steeper and pretty much fun. Then, when you hit your forties and fifties time's going a lot faster and things are starting to get a little scary. After that it seems like the sled is screaming along, almost straight down the mountain, and all you can do is hold on fast. Well, that's what I'm doing right now… holding on fast. But I have to say it's been one hell of a ride! I have no regrets!

I went to kindergarten at St. Mary's School. My wife and I, we just got back from a fifty-year high school reunion. Fifty years. I can't believe it's gone this fast. I started school around 1945, right around the end of the Second World War.

I remember going to the movies. They cost about a nickel. And movies were such a big part of my life. I still remember some of the old dialogue from some of those movies: Van Johnson, Liz Taylor. Evel Knievel told me you get to a point in your life when all you want to do is make love to Elizabeth Taylor, and then, if you ever do get the chance, it won't make any difference because you'll be too old.

There's a quick story about Evel. He came to be on my show with me one day and he had on a red, white, and blue shirt with stars on the shoulders. I said, "Evel, that's a beautiful shirt." And without missing a beat he said, "You'll have one just like it the day after tomorrow." And sure enough, two days later in the mail, from Evel Knievel, I got a red, white, and blue sport shirt with stars on it. What a great guy. What a great life he's had.

Anyway, back to kindergarten in Ottumwa at St. Mary's. For some reason I could never understand, I started to think about things up in the sky. In the summertime we used to lay out in the backyard, my buddies and I, up on Market Street, and look up at the sky and talk about what was out there and where the planets were and see shooting stars and wonder what it was all about. I took an interest in life on other planets and what that was all about. Remember, this is way back in the mid-1940s, before Roswell and before all the science fiction movies of the fifties. But for some reason I started to draw pictures of ships that looked like flying saucers. They had the beams of light and domes and the crescent shape and everything. And I remember in second grade Sister Dolores said, "What are you drawing there?" And she took all the pictures of the space ships I'd drawn as a seven-year-old kid. The nuns thought this was just crazy. Why was this kid sitting around drawing pictures of crazy-looking space ships? But I still think that maybe there is life out there and they visited us and that I'm part of it. I wonder if I'm some kind of "Hybrid." In fact, with some of the UFO experts I had on the show, if we really hit it off, I'd always ask them if they were a "Hybrid." And a lot of the time they'd look up at me with surprise and say, "Yeah, I am." It's like we were bred here by aliens or something. Or not.

So anyway, when the 1950s rolled around, I'd go to all the flying saucer movies. *The Day the Earth Stood Still* is the best one ever made. *"Gort! Klaatu barada nikto!"* and *"Gort! Barenga!"* God, I loved that stuff. I think it's still so popular because it speaks to a wish I think all of us have -- that some all-powerful force will come to the Earth and stop all the wars and the fighting, keep us from blowing ourselves up.

There was also *The Thing* with James Arness, which scared the hell out of everybody. The kids spread the rumor, "When the Thing stuck his hand through the door, thirteen people fainted!" James Arness came to town one time and he did a telethon for KTVO, the TV station. He's a great big guy – about six-foot eight. He played the part of the Thing in that movie. Then he went on to play Sheriff Matt Dillon in *Gunsmoke*, one of the early and greatest TV Westerns.

GISELLE MASSI

I had probably thousands of guests in the course if my radio career – on KCMO it was twenty-five years, on KMBZ, where I had greater success, it was ten years. But in the twenty-five years of doing guests on talk, I only had, after I retired, two or three that have contacted me, and they've all been women. And I probably had ten thousand people to pass through the portals of the Mike Murphy show, and one that I stayed in contact with after I left was Giselle Massi.

She had written a book called: *We are Here for a Purpose: HOW TO FIND YOURS.* The producers had called to say there's a woman named Giselle Massi, and she talks to her father every day, and I said, "That wouldn't be any good. Why would I want to talk about that?" And they said, "Well, her father's been dead for twenty years."

Well, she wrote a book, and it was a little purple book about living and dying, so I had her on one day, and it was just magic. I don't know what happened, but something came through the microphone and into the radio that I've never experienced before. And she said she was gonna do a book signing at Borders, I think it was, and I thought, "Well, I don't know if anybody will show up for something like this because, you know, it was different and strange and paranormal and all that."

And so she left the studio, and I wondered about how many people would show up, if anybody, and I felt sorry for her. A good looking girl, she'd been the editor of the *Denver Post's* Entertainment Section.

And the next day somebody called me, and I asked them, "Did anybody go to the book signing for Giselle Massi?" And a guy called me and he said, "You know, for some reason something struck me as being really bizarre about her interview on your show and I went to the book signing, and there was a line that went around the block. They were until ten o'clock that night waiting to talk to her."

I don't know what that was, but some kind of magic happened. It was the biggest crowd they'd ever had for a book signing, and she said, "I couldn't believe it, when the people started to come they never quit." And she said that finally they had to close the store, and they were still standing in line.

She was a great woman, and I still talk to her. Giselle Massi.

TALK SHOW HOSTS: TOM SNYDER, JACK PAAR, MIKE DOUGLAS, AND MERV GRIFFIN

Tom Snyder, one of the great talk show hosts, recently passed away. I always enjoyed watching him; he was an immensely curious man, and he refused to dumb down himself, his guests, or his audience, to fit some conventional stereotype of what television should be or what the audience would appreciate. His honest, friendly attitude with his guests allowed them to relax and be themselves. He was the first American talk show host to interview John Lennon in 1975.

Another great one was Jack Paar, but maybe the best of them all was Mike Douglas. A lot of people don't know Mike started out as a singer, working with Kay Kaiser's band. He was also the singing voice of Prince Charming in Walt Disney's *Cinderella*. When he came on the show he was one of the nicest people I ever met. *The Mike Douglas Show* aired its first Philadelphia-based show on August 30, 1965. Guests ranged from Truman Capote and Richard Nixon to the Rolling Stones, Herman's Hermits and the Turtles. The show helped introduce entertainers such as Barbra Streisand and Aretha Franklin. By 1967, *The Mike Douglas Show* was broadcast to 171 markets and 6 million people.

Then there's Merv Griffin. Merv was so big and so rich – he produced so many of those game shows – and so nice, I was nervous about having him on. So about five minutes into our session, during a break, I said, "How we doing?" He said, "This is going great. You are really good at this." Now *that's* a compliment!

THE CATTLE DRIVE

YEAR ONE

I don't want to take all the credit for this. One day I had a guy on the show with me, Dick Ray, the Master Plumber. He said, "You know what Kansas City ought to do? They ought to have a cattle drive. Drive a herd of cattle through downtown Kansas City." And I thought, "Boy, that's a great idea."

So about a year later I thought, "You know, I'm gonna do this cattle drive." So I called my friends out at Benjamin Ranch, Bob Faulkner and Howard Benjamin, and said, "Do you think there's any chance we could pull something like this off? Can we put this together?" They said, "Well, yeah, we can getcha some steers." So I said, "Well, let's try and do something." They said okay. I said, "How many steers can you get?" They said, "Oh, eight or nine." And I thought, "Well, that's not a bad start."

So the plan was, on April Fool's Day we get the steers down in front of the Italian Gardens, owned by Carl DiCapo, who's been my great friend all these years. And Carl said, "Sure, we can start it from here." And I started promoting it on the air as "Kansas City's First Cattle Drive in a

Hundred Years." The city had outlawed cattle drives just like they did St. Patrick's Day.

Anyway, we all met down at the Italian Gardens and we had a great crowd. A whole lotta people and at least eight steers, and we went from the Italian Gardens, down Baltimore, then over to Main Street, and on up to the Hereford House on 20th St. CBS News picked it up and the Weather Channel, too. They said, "Can you imagine driving a herd of cattle down to the Hereford House where they're gonna kill 'em and eat 'em?" Of course that didn't happen, and it was a really neat deal. Because it was April 1, everybody just thought it was an April Fool's joke. But that was just year one. Lucky for us someone took a photo of one steer mounting another so we had some great artwork to put on the commemorative t-shirt for next year's event. I think they're still floating around town.

YEAR TWO

So that was the first Cattle Drive, and I'm thinking, "Boy, we've really got something going on here. Maybe it's time for an encore." A guy called me out of the blue and said, "I loved your cattle drive. Do you know who I know?" And I said, "No, who?" He said, "I know Dale Robertson." Now Dale Robertson was a genuine cowboy, born in Oklahoma, handsome as a prince, played in tons of westerns, and he succeeded Ronald Reagan on the TV series *Death Valley Days*.

So this guy says, "I know Dale, and I bet I could get him to come to this cattle drive next time." And I'm thinking, "Boy, this is really gonna be good." And sure enough, Dale Robertson says, 'Yeah, I'll come. It sounds like fun."

So Dale Robertson comes to town and we all meet down at the Italian Gardens the night before and we have a "Pre-Cattle Drive Party."

In the meantime, I'd called my buddies at Benjamin Stables, Bob Faulkner and Howard Benjamin, and said, "I wanna really go all out this year. Can you guys find and bring in a hundred longhorn steers?" They said, "Well, it won't be easy, but we think we can do it." And sure enough, they came up with a hundred longhorn steers and parked the trucks down in front of the Italian Gardens.

At eleven o'clock the next morning we had a hundred longhorn steers, all in pens that we'd made for them. Dale Robertson is there with me and Carl DiCapo and we're saying, "This is gonna be great!" Claire McCaskill came and the mayor was there. It was just a major event in this town and everyone was really excited.

Howard Benjamin had told me, "Mike, I want you to ride Warpaint." Warpaint was the most famous horse this town has ever seen. He was the stallion who the Indian brave rode as a mascot at the Chief's games. The horse I rode in the first cattle drive was named "Lucky," and he died.

So I get on Warpaint. We get all the cattle ready. We take off. I say, "Head 'em up, move 'em out, let's go!" And the longhorns take off running and all of a sudden we've got a stampede on our hands.

I said to Bob Faulkner, "What's going on? What do we do?" They're all loose on the streets of downtown Kansas City, running wherever they wanted. They ended up on the top floor of the City Hall, in parking garages, in hotels, it was chaos. *The Kansas City Star* quoted a man who'd come out of the Muhlebach Hotel and he said, "You know, I'm looking at this and saying to myself, 'You wouldn't see this in Boston or anywhere else.'"

So that was the second cattle drive and it was a total mess and most people said this was the most fun they'd ever had in their lives. I think we even rounded up all the cattle… eventually. I hope.

YEARS THREE PLUS

Some more on the cattle drives. I think we did five. Then the station got sold. But we were getting ten to fifteen thousand people showing up each year, and I thought it was gonna be another St. Patrick's Day Parade. And it might've been. But the city – the bluebloods – never liked the "Cowtown" image. But that was what we were. A cowtown and a railroad town.

That's what made Kansas City great. That was our heritage. And I thought the Cattle Drive would be something really special that would help us celebrate our history.

But they decided they didn't want to associate with that, so we skipped a year and decided to try and do it in Mission, Kansas. And that worked and became great. We did two or three on Johnson Drive in Mission and we were getting fifteen or twenty thousand each time. It was a blast.

One time we brought Alex Karras down to be part of it. Alex Karras was an All-American tackle at the University of Iowa who went on to become one of the greatest NFL defensive tackles of all time with the Detroit Lions. He'd also done some acting work. He was in a sitcom called *Webster* and was pretty famous for playing "Mongo" in *Blazing Saddles*. The classic scene in the movie was when Alex, always a big, strong, muscular guy, knocked out a horse with one punch.

So we called Alex and he said he'd come in and be the Grand Marshal of the Cattle Drive. He came to town and stayed with my great friend, Larry Stewart, who, after he died, was revealed to be Kansas City's "Secret Santa." Every year around Christmas he'd put on a Santa suit and drive around town giving out thousands of dollars – in twenties, fifties, hundreds – to the folks in the less fortunate parts of the city.

The night before the drive, Larry and Alex and myself and others had a "fart in the fire" contest. We were paying tribute to that great scene in *Blazing Saddles* where the cowboys, having eaten lots of baked beans, sat around the campfire farting. It was really a classic. I think it was the first movie anybody ever farted in.

So the next day we had a great cattle drive and we were really starting to bring in the stars, like Dale Robertson and Alex Karras. For the one next year, we'd called Clint Eastwood and he said he'd be happy to come. But it turned out, for whatever reasons, they decided to quit having the cattle drives. We sure gave it a run while it lasted.

CO-AUTHOR'S NOTE: I'm a New York kid who's lived in Philadelphia, Chicago, Los Angeles, and Houston, to name a few. All big cities. But never in my life have I heard of anything more outrageous and spectacular than the running of a herd of longhorn steers through the streets of a major city in a cattle drive. Totally unbelievable! It makes me proud.

GEORGE GOBEL'S ONE-LINER

Working in Kansas City, it was always a challenge to get celebrities to come on the morning show. Back in the fifties in Ottumwa, we were too poor to have a TV. We'd just have to listen to the radio. But I remember my classmates at school, who did have TVs, always talking about *The George Gobel Show* and how funny this guy was. How he'd talk about his "spooky old wife, Alice," and say, "Well, then, there, now." I think one of his most famous lines came on the Johnny Carson show one night when he said to Johnny, "Do you ever get the feeling the world is a tuxedo and you're a pair of brown shoes?"

Well, one day I finally got to have George come on the show, but what I remember most about him is our conversation *before* he went on. Now remember, George had a reputation of having a cocktail or two once in a while, but this is like eight o'clock in the morning! George pulls me aside and whispers, "You don't have any whiskey around here, do you?" I said, "No, I don't think we do." He says, "You don't have anything around here to drink?" I said, "Sorry, I'm pretty sure we don't." Then he looks at me real close with those squinty little eyes and says, "You mean you go out there *alone*?"

GEORGE CARLIN

I always thought George Carlin was one of the most talented, creative comedians who ever lived. I watched his shows on HBO and they were always funny and insightful. He was such an iconoclast.

When I first started doing the show on KCMO, George was one of my first guests. I was really new to this live interviewing thing and didn't know what I was doing. (Still don't!)

It turned out I was the thirty-ninth interview he'd done that day. Or maybe the forty-third or the sixty-eighth. Anyway, it was the end of the day and he'd done all these interviews and was probably pretty tired. I was always interested that he was one of the first guys to wear ponytails, back in the early eighties. At least he was one of the first I'd seen. So when the interview started I said, "What are you doing now with your hair?" He said, "Mike, is that it?" I said, "What?" He said, "Is that all?" I said, "I guess." He said, "Bye." Maybe I should've opened with a different question.

FOR RICHER OR POORER

In the beginning of this business it was always about money. And when I got to Springfield, Illinois, after working in Ottumwa, Iowa ("1480 on your radio dial"), everybody knew what everybody was making and they were always talking about what people were making in St. Louis and what they were making in Chicago. When we moved to Springfield around 1960, we were making maybe eighty bucks a week, but we heard in St. Louis they were making a hundred and ninety! So we all started setting our sights on the bigger towns and cities. The bigger markets, as they call them in radio.

So when I got a call to go to Moline, that was two hundred a week and that was just a big jump. I got to thinking what I was making in Ottumwa, sixty dollars a week, and the way inflation went over time and the way the pay scales changed. There I was making sixty a week in Ottumwa and the best year I ever had a few years later I was making six thousand a week! What an industry! People could go from rags to riches and back again in the blink of an eye.

Moline was one of the Quad Cities (Bettendorf, Iowa; Davenport, Iowa; and Rock Island, Illinois, were the other three). All my friends were going to school at St. Ambrose College in Davenport, which is where I should have probably gone.

Anyway, when Moline called, a man named G. Laverne Flambo thought I was somethin'. He didn't know what, but he thought I was somethin'. In fact he told me that one day. He said, "You know, I know you're somethin' but I don't know what you are."

So he took a liking to me and I liked him. They called him "Mr. Show Business." He brought in touring acts to the Black Hawk Theater, I think it was. He brought in Phyllis Diller, and I saw her the first time when she premiered. And he brought Dick Clark, and we had a nice time with him.

So Flambo thought I was "his boy," and he put me on afternoons on WQUA and I did pretty good there and had a good time. Then they bought a station in Indianapolis and they sent me there. I got fired three years later and went back to Moline to work with Flambo. Then three months later was when I came to Kansas City.

WILD LOBSTERS

This St. Patrick's Day 2008 is the thirty-fifth anniversary of the first parade in 1973 and I'm thinking about all the memories I have. And one of the best ones is with Pat O'Neill, Dan Hogerty, Cy Perkins, Jim Lynch, and their families. After the parade we'd all get together and have dinner somewhere.

One year Cy said, "Why don't you all come to my house and we'll get some lobsters?" So Pat O'Neill said, "I'll go to the Savoy and get the lobsters live out of the tank and bring them to your house."

So Pat went to the Savoy and got about twenty live lobsters and we went to Cy's house to put on the pots to cook 'em. And about an hour and a half later we're saying, "Where the hell is O'Neill and the lobsters?" Finally Pat calls on his phone and screams, "The lobsters have all gotten loose. They're crawling all over the place! They're on the seat, the floor, my lap, my face, they're attacking me." He said, "I can't catch 'em all. They're really dangerous!"

Well, about two hours later Pat pulls up with a car full of angry lobsters and we've all been drinking all day, it's ten o'clock at night, and Kelly Perkins, Cy's wife, said, "I'll cook 'em!" So she boiled 'em all and we sat down about eleven o'clock, after a real long St. Patrick's Day, with the lobsters and our bowls of hot melted butter.

We were having trouble getting the shells off and we started cracking them and hitting at them with our fists and Cy had a lobster that had butter on it and shot a stream of boiling hot butter into the eyes of Jean O'Neill, Pat's wife. She started screaming that she thought she'd gone blind. But things calmed down and everyone relaxed, but it was a pretty tough night for the O'Neills, first with Pat and the lobster attack, then with Jean and the butter in the eyes.

Just another wild day in the history of St. Patrick's Day in Kansas City.

JOHN GARY

John Gary had one of the most beautiful tenor voices and was one of the "prettiest" men who ever lived. He recorded twenty-three albums and was a popular guest on late night TV shows, from Jack Paar to Steve Allen to Johnny Carson.

He came to town one time and we had a nice visit. I became a great fan and I stayed in touch with him for several years. I called him one day while I was on the air and said, "John, we haven't talked for a while. I thought you might like to tell the listeners about your latest album and what you're doing with your life and so on." He said, "Well, I don't know whether I can talk about it now." I said, "Whattaya mean?" He said, "Well, Mike, I'm dying." And I said, "Oh, no!" That's hard to take anytime, but especially when you're on the air with an old friend. I felt just terrible.

So John said, "Maybe you can call me down the road and I'll talk some more to you." But that was the last time I ever talked to him.

I thought he did the absolute best version of "Danny Boy" that'd ever been done. Every year before St. Patrick's Day I'd have this contest, "Who could sing the best 'Danny Boy,'" and it was always won by John Gary.

THE ODD SQUAD

I started a thing – I guess you'd call it a thing, or a club or a group or something – called "The Odd Squad." Remember back in the late sixties there was this show called *The Mod Squad*, a police show with Tige Andrews, Peggy Lipton, Clarence Williams, and Michael Cole. It was one of the hottest shows going.

I used to ask my brother, Pat, I said, "Brother, why do you think people like us?" He said, "Because we're so damned odd." So we weren't weird, we were just odd. And most of our family was odd.

So I thought it might be fun to get a group of people together around here and call it "The Odd Squad," people who'd go around searching for "odd" things. So I went to a guy who had a car dealership and he said, "I've got a car I'll give to you, it's got four-wheel drive and everything, and we can put a siren on top of it. We can call it 'The Odd Squad Squad Car.'" I was Major Murphy in The Odd Squad.

I had a guy who orchestrated our liberation of Paola, Kansas, whose name was Billy Rigger, but I called him Billy Whipple. Why? I don't know. Just odd I guess. So we got together and we had "Odd Squad" membership cards made up. It said, "This card authorizes bearer to investigate anything ODD." And we had five or ten thousand of those cards we gave out. And there are still people who come up to me and say, "Look at this." And they show me their Odd Squad membership card.

Later, my brother and I were doing our TV show in our monks' robes called "Murphy's Monstrous Movie Show." And when Tige Andrews came to town, my old buddy, Pat O'Neill, gets him to come on our show. The head of *The Mod Squad* meets the men of The Odd Squad.

LARRY KING

While I was working at KMBZ we were all such good buddies, we were all riding the great wave of success. KMBR was the only other station in the building and the manager of it was a man named Joe Abernathy. Joe was the most charismatic guy I ever knew.

Well, Joe got an offer to go to a station in Miami called WIOD and he did. It stood for Wonderful Isle of Dreams. And there for many years was a man on the microphone named Larry King. And Larry was the number one radio personality in Miami for years. He got to be a good friend of Jackie Gleason. He did his show on remote from Pumpernik's Restaurant in Miami Beach.

Everybody loved Larry King. He had his radio show, wrote a newspaper column, and got to be real popular, but he got into some kind of financial trouble with some other people and got fired.

He kind of disappeared from sight and this Joe Abernathy wanted me to come down and work at WIOD. So we flew down one weekend and Joe said, "Listen, if I can get you to come down here and work at WIOD, I'll bring back Larry King. If you work here, I'll find out where Larry is and bring him back."

Well, we flew back to Kansas City and decided we didn't want to live in Miami.

And that was that until about seven years later when I had Larry King on the air with me and I said, "Larry, tell me about this man, Joe Abernathy." And Larry proceeded to tell me about how Joe tracked him down and brought him back to WIOD and Larry would give Joe his check every week because Joe knew Larry was kind of a compulsive spender and he'd spend whatever money he had, so Joe gave it to Larry in small amounts and helped him budget it.

So Larry and I and Joe became this triumvirate of friends and whenever I had Larry on my show in Kansas City, he would tell stories about Joe Abernathy.

One time Larry told me a story about being at the horse track and he had almost no money to his name – maybe forty or fifty dollars; he tipped the valet who parked his car, so now he's down to thirty-five or forty dollars. When he gets into the clubhouse, he looks at the program and sees a horse that has the same name as his sister, another had something to do with his birthday, and another tied in with the date, and he put the last of his money on those three horses. He put some money on a trifecta, some on an exacta, and the rest on a long shot. And they all came in. Now he's telling me this story on the air and I'm thinking, "This is the greatest story I ever heard. Guy's got almost no money to his name and puts it all on horses and they all come in."

The track gave him a check – I think it was nineteen or twenty thousand dollars. And he goes from being broke to having about twenty thousand dollars in one horse race. What a story. I think I would rate Larry King as the most fun guest I ever had on the show.

TINY TIM

I used to have certain people on that I started calling the "Odd Squad." They were interesting, wonderful people most of the time, but they were just... well, kind of "odd." And when I try to think of the oddest one of all, I guess it was Tiny Tim.

Tiny Tim – his real name was Herbert Khaury – was a true music expert, who knew almost every song from the late 1800s through the 1940s. He started singing and playing his ukulele around Harvard University as a street musician and he was quite a hit, but soon he moved to New York and before long was booked on *Rowan and Martin's Laugh-In*.

His song, "Tiptoe Through the Tulips" became an immediate sensation and so did he. When he came to Kansas City he performed at the Playboy Club and I met him in the lobby. The first thing he said was, "Guess what? I just got served papers from Miss Vicki and she's divorcing me!" But he still invited us to his show.

I didn't hear from him till many years later when he came back to Kansas City and gladly agreed to come on the show. When he got there, he said, "Mr. Murphy, could I please use the bathroom?" And I said, "Of course." So he went in there and when it got time to go on the air, he still hadn't come out. So I went in and he said, "I'm very nervous about doing this. Would you have any whiskey?" I said, "Let me see."

So I went up to the boss's office and I said, "You got any whiskey?" And he says, "Yeah, I got a whole bottle of something around here someplace." So I brought the bottle back down to Tiny, who was still in the bathroom, and gave it to him. After a few minutes, he still wasn't coming out. So I went back in and he'd had about half of that bottle. We finally got him to come out and he came on the show and was terrific. He knew every song from every era and he played his ukulele some and we just had a wonderful time.

Well, I didn't see him for a long time until one time I was in Omaha at the race track and he was performing at the Nebraska State Fair. Well, somebody brought him to the track and I saw him sitting there alone and I went over and he remembered me. I said, "Tiny, are you all right?" And he said, "Well, I haven't had anything to eat and I don't have any money." So I bought him a big prime rib sandwich and I said, "Tiny, I'm gonna put a bet down on a horse for you." Well, the horse won and I brought him back the winnings – sixty or seventy bucks -- and gave it to him and Tiny and I became thicker than thieves. Over the years we kept in touch. He was a blessed soul. And the end of this story is actually the end of Tiny Tim. One night he got on stage in Des Moines or someplace, his last show. He sang "Tiptoe Through the Tulips" one last time and then just up and died. What a wonderful human being he was.

PEOPLE AND PLACES

I thought that while I was writing this book it might be fun to go around to some of the places in Kansas City I've haunted – or that have haunted me – through the years. Madeleine Albright, one of our great secretaries of state and just a wonderful person, came on the show one time. In the midst of our visit she said, "I just heard you do a commercial for the Salty Iguana. That sounds like a really great place. When I come to town the next time would you take me to the Salty Iguana?" I said, "Well, sure!"

So a couple of weeks later I got a nice letter from her and she said, "It was sure nice to be on your show. And by the way, about that Salty Iguana. When I come to town would you take me there?" And I said to myself, "Don't mind if I do." And one of these days we just might get there.

O'Neill's

Anyway, we've done a whole lotta chapters for this book there, and a couple at Jasper's, a couple at the Corner Cocktail, and a couple at O'Neill's, one of the great local Irish restaurants. I kind of helped kick O'Neill's off on a St. Patrick's Day a few years ago and we had the Elders there and it was a great day.

Jasper's

One of my all-time favorite restaurants is Jasper's out on 103rd Street in the Watts Mill Shopping Center. As far as I know Jasper's is still the only five-star restaurant in Kansas City. Well, before the show at Kelly's, I must have had four or five "last shows" at Jasper's. I go there for lunch, to record stories for this book, and even now, I still sit in with Jasper Junior ("J.J.") on his popular Saturday morning radio show every once in a while.

There was always quite a turnout at Jasper's for my "last shows." Ex-Kansas City mayors – Wheeler, Cleaver, and Barnes – Marilyn Maye, Nathan Granner. Nathan is one of the "American Tenors" and he'd come and sing opera, and let me tell you, there's something really magic about hearing a great tenor singing opera in a great Italian restaurant.

I remember when TWA was based in Kansas City, the pilots, when they were flying over Kansas City, would offer the passengers parachutes in case someone wanted to jump out and go to Jasper's, their favorite restaurant.

David Schoenstadt was a doctor, owner of the Kansas City Comets and one of my great friends. I had kind of networked this deal for him that got him a million dollars, and he, in return, gave me a "finder's fee" of $60,000.

Well, I wanted to thank him by taking him to Jasper's for dinner along with the couple who were the other part of the deal, the lenders of the money. So that was it. On a special occasion, you went to Jasper's.

So David was kind of a free spirit, he always wore Levi's no matter what. And I said, "David, when we go to Jasper's, you gotta wear a coat and tie." (That may have changed, but back then that was the dress code.) So I figured for once he'd dress up a bit.

When he got there, David gets out of his car and is wearing a nice sport coat, a fancy silk tie… and Levi's! Well, we went in and J.J. said no problem. But that was David Schoenstadt… a true iconoclast to the end.

BRANSON

I wanted to do some stories about the shorter trips I've taken closer to home. Some of the best were some of the simplest and closest to home. One of these trips was to Branson.

We went to Branson at the height of Branson's popularity, when it was really starting to take off. All these great stars from Las Vegas were opening shows in this little town in southern Missouri. Andy Williams, Glen Campbell, Jim Stafford, the Gatlin Brothers, Yakov Smirnoff, Conway Twitty. So I decided I'd go to Branson and do the radio show from there for a week.

We were gonna do the show from several theaters: Ray Stevens was one and Jim Stafford was another. The one I liked best was Boxcar Willie. And Boxcar Willie and I became great friends. He'd been a disc jockey before in Texas. He said to me, "You come to my theater and do your show from there and I'll introduce you to some of my friends and we'll have a good time."

So we did that. The first show I did from Boxcar Willie's theater, just Boxcar was the guest. But he said, "Andy Williams is a good friend of mine. We'll go to his theater and do a show from there." So I said, "Yeah, that'll be great!"

Now Andy Williams had a beautiful theater. So we get there to do the show from Andy Williams' theater and we had a bunch of guests lined up: Jim Stafford, Mel Tillis, and Ray Stevens of "Ahab the Arab" fame. But nobody showed up. So Boxcar Willie said, "Let me call Mel Tillis."

So he called Mel Tillis and Mel came over and we had a good time with Mel. And Mel said, "I'll tell you what. I've got a place down here and we've got a great restaurant and bar over there called the Mole Hole. You can come over and do the next show from over there if you want." I said, "That'd be neat."

And then Andy Williams came in and said, "I'll be on your show." Andy was a great guy. I'd had him on the radio show before. He was a good Iowa guy, from Wall Lake. Andy was wearing some kind of robe, so the first thing I said to him was, "Andy, you're not the kind of guy that'd go around with his robe open, are ya'?" He got a kick out of that.

So there was Mel Tillis, Boxcar Willie, Andy Williams, Ray Stevens, and me and we had a great, great time. If you ever go to Branson, be sure you go to the Andy Williams Theater. If you get to talk to Andy, say, "Andy, you remember Mike Murphy being down here?" I bet he would.

I had all those great guests, but one I really wanted was Conway Twitty. They told me, "Conway Twitty doesn't do interviews." But somebody got to him, I think it was Boxcar Willie, and he said, "Go on with Murphy. He's a great guy." And sure enough, Conway called our producer and said, "I'm gonna come on there with him."

And he showed up and said, "I'm going on with you." And I said, "That's neat. It's great of you to come on the show with me."

Conway said, "You know what?" I said, "No, what?" He said, "I will have only done two interviews. I did Tom Snyder and now I'm doing you. And that's all I'm gonna do." And sure enough, he did Tom Snyder and me. He never did do another interview. He actually died in Branson in 1993 from an aortic aneurysm.

When I was a disc jockey back in Ottumwa, Conway had a huge hit called "It's Only Make Believe." It was a terrific song and an enormous hit. He told me the story of how he got his name. He was driving along toward Oklahoma, I think, and he saw a road sign that said Conway, Arkansas. The next sign he saw was Twitty, Oklahoma. His real name was Harold Lloyd Jenkins, so I guess he thought Conway Twitty was a better name for a singer. I think he was right. And he sure was one heck of a singer.

DR. JOYCE BROTHERS

Dr. Joyce Brothers became one of the most famous people in America. She started out by being a guest on *The $64,000 Question* game show. She had become an expert on the subject of boxing, but as it turned out she really didn't know that much about the sport, but she was a popular contestant, so the people of the show got her some tutoring.

Well, she went on to win the *$64,000 Question* and started appearing on talk shows and writing books and became quite the famous expert on things. So she'd written her last book – got about two million dollars for it – and she was out on tour promoting it. Well, she got to my show.

I said, "How you doing?" She said, "Fine. Well, not really, can I use your bathroom?" I said, "Sure, it's right down the hall there." So she goes to the bathroom… and what do you suppose? She never came back. I never saw her again. I must've been at the tail end of the tour.

The disappearing doctor Joyce Brothers.

DR. JOHN E. MACK

This'll be just a little story, not a long story, but maybe the best segment of this book. I had a man on, a man named Dr. John Mack, and he was a professor of psychiatry at Harvard. He had begun hypnotic regression with people who had had UFO experiences and had completed around eighteen of these.

He wrote a couple of books based on his observations, which caused him some problems with the administrators at Harvard, but it got resolved and eventually an institute was established in his honor, the John E. Mack Institute. So I had him on the show; he's just a great, wonderful guy. I really liked him and he told me stories about the people he had regressed.

Then he did a personal appearance at Unity Temple and my wife, Cathy, and daughter Susan went to see him. When they met him, they told him who they were and he said what a great experience he had being on the show with me. So we became kind of friends. I'd have him on from time to time on the phone and then I had him on again in the studio. He was just a really brilliant man.

So a couple of years ago the news came out that a Dr. John Mack had been run over and killed in London at about midnight by a drunk driver.

So John Mack was dead. Then six months later it came out that on the very same night, another man named John Mack was also run over and killed by a drunken motorist, in London and at the very same time. Two John Macks are run down and killed by drunks on the same night in the same city. Explain that! Is that too weird, or what? Now what do you suppose was behind that?

Was it pure coincidence or did someone think he was telling too many stories about UFOs, aliens, hybrids, and other phenomena?

If you're interested in seeing what all the fuss was about, pick up: *Abduction: Human Encounters with Aliens* or *Passport to the Cosmos: Human Transformation and Alien Encounters*. And remember, these were written by a professor of psychiatry at Harvard.

.

OVER THE RAINBOW

In Kansas City, in the seventies, the thing to do was to go to Omaha. Omaha's a great town and they have a wonderful steak house there called Ross's. They'd have prime rib and T-bones and lobster… It was just a great place to eat. We'd drive up there on a Friday and come back on Sunday and it was always a fantastic time. We'd go to the horse track named Ak-Sar-Ben. A friend of mine had lived here for twenty years and always thought that Ak-Sar-Ben was some kind of fancy stable in Arabia where they bred Arabian stallions. You should've seen his face when I told him that Ak-Sar-Ben was just Nebraska spelled backwards! Anyway, people from Kansas City would go to Ak-Sar-Ben in droves to see the horse races and do a little "betting on the ponies" and have a marvelous time.

One time I was there and there was this bet you could make called a "Pick Six" and you had to pick the winners of six races in a row. There was $75,000 in the pot and I made a bet and won it! Since there were four other people who'd picked those horses we had to divide it so I only won $15,000 but that was the biggest win I ever had at Ak-Sar-Ben. After that we really started following the horses and went to tracks all over the country. We got pretty good at it, too.

One of the places we went was Phoenix and they have a great track called Turf Paradise. What made it really good was that a lot of the people who went there were elderly and didn't have that much experience handicapping horses. That often made the payoffs unusually good. They'd just come out for fun. They'd bet their sister's birthday or their kids' anniversaries, whatever. They'd have a lot of fun and they'd get their share of wins, too.

So we got out there one day and found a horse named "Over the Rainbow" was running and it was going off at 80-1! Well those odds are usually the sign of a real nag and it'd be a dumb bet because those long shots almost never come in. But because it was called "Over the Rainbow," and because we were from Kansas, we thought it might be some kind of special sign from above. So we put $50 on its nose, $30 to place and $20 to show, plus we played all the combination bets like exactas and such, my wife and I both.

So when the race started, the darn thing came out of the gate and got in the lead and held it all the way to the home stretch. Old Over the Rainbow was now ten lengths in the lead and nobody was gonna beat him that day! So he came in first, our place horse placed, our show horse showed, all our combo bets paid too. I think we won something over $20,000 that day on that one race. They said, "Do you want it in a check?" I said, "No, I want it in cash." So I had all this money in all of my pockets, my billfold, my wife's purse, everywhere. And when we walked out we were tipping all the attendants big time.

There was this woman who'd waited on us in the clubhouse and I gave her a $200 tip. She got down on her knees and started to cry. She said, "Last night, before all this went on today, I prayed to the Lord that something good would happen. I needed this money so bad. I was totally broke. I didn't have a nickel. You can't imagine how much this means to me." So I think about gambling and that if you're gonna gamble and you win and you give some of it away, well, that's what it's all about.

BRUCE BUREMAN

There are just a couple of things I'd like to say about being on the air with Mike Murphy. It was so incredibly easy to be on with Mike Murphy because nobody interviewed people better and no one made it easier. The trick about being on the radio is making it sound easy. And it ain't!

It's an honor to be associated with him. In fact, we did a home repair show for four or five years and I've never laughed so hard or so often. There were three or four other crazy people in the studio and we would tell stories and maybe take only two or three calls in an hour. We called it "The Stupid Show." Because it was.

But it was always fun, and Mike made it very, very easy and it's an honor to be his friend.

THE INCREDIBLE BURNING MAN

This is an amazing story. I had this man on my program several times. He came into town recently so we asked him to tell the story in his own words.

This is Captain George Burke, Air Force Retired, plane crash and burn survivor, sole survivor of military plane crash.

After coming back from Vietnam, this happened 4 May 1970 in Northern California. I was piloting an aircraft with fourteen passengers on board, heading for Fairchild Air Force Base in Spokane and shortly after take-off we were at three thousand feet when we had rapid decompression and massive structural failure. I remember the sequence of the crash, but I do not remember anything else for a long time afterward, including being on fire. A rancher found me while I was burning. Later that day I was transported by C-141 aircraft to San Antonio, Texas, where I spent eighty-nine days in the Army Institute of Surgical Research Burn Unit and spent a total time of eighteen months in the hospital.

I've been fortunate and blessed to be on Mike Murphy's show seven times, four in-studio and three remote. How I met Mike Murphy was this: I had become one of his many, many fans over the years. I was returning from Phoenix, Arizona, in 1994. I had lived there before as an assistant professor at Arizona State University. I had flown out there to meet some people and get the lay of the land, so to speak, and look for a house.

I was coming back and I was getting ready to board an America West flight from Phoenix to Kansas City. As I approached the ticket counter, I heard a very familiar voice. I walked up to the gentleman who was standing talking to the ramp agent and said, "It's about time you get back to Kansas City. Your fans miss you." When he turned around I saw it really was Mike Murphy. He said, "Who are you? How do you know me? Where are you from? Where are you going?" What ensued thereafter became a very nice relationship. I have a great deal of respect for Mike. I call him "Roy Hobbs," from the movie The Natural, *implying that he's "the best there ever was or ever will be."*

We flew on the plane coming back to Kansas City. As we walked down the jetway to the aircraft, he was asking me what I do, what I did. And I told him the story of the plane crash and being burned and my recovery. After the plane took off, he moved up to the front part of the aircraft and we sat and talked for about two and a half hours about my experiences in detail. He asked me many questions: "Are you nervous about getting on an airplane?" "How do you feel, what do you do?"

And then again at baggage claim at KCI when we were parting he pointed his index finger at me and said, "You make sure you call my producer tomorrow morning. I want to have you on our show."

The next day I called Mike's producer. They were in the studio in Westwood, and within a matter of a week I was on his program for at least an hour. What followed after that were three more in-studio interviews and three more remotes from my home in Scottsdale, Arizona. The most recent one was in the year 2000, which would be the thirtieth anniversary of my plane crash. I've enjoyed knowing Mike. He's an institution in Kansas City. I miss him, I like him, and I respect him. I'm very glad I walked up to him that day in 1994 and introduced myself. It's been a real blessing for me to have been on his program and I've enjoyed every minute of it.

It was a pleasure, Mike.

George Burke, the Incredible Burning Man. He was the only survivor of that crash in 1970. I've always thought it was fascinating about people who are "only survivors" of tragedies like plane crashes. They always go around asking, Why me? Why was I spared? Do I have some special purpose in life? It really changes them. And it's affected George that way.

He told me that right before the crash, or right at the time of the crash, time stopped and stood still. And the pilot and co-pilot appeared to him in the doorway of the craft and said, "It's okay. It's all right." Of course, they were dead. And during this ordeal, George himself "died on the table" twice.

George was thrown from the plane and was lying on the ground and his body was actually on fire, from the inside. His insides were burning. Smoke was coming out his nose, his mouth, and his ears. George was in the hospital for eighteen months, his wife divorced him, but he later met and married a beautiful young lady from Kansas City and they are living happily ever after in Phoenix, Arizona.

George Burke, the Incredible Burning Man.

THE VANISHING HORSES

When we went to Cedar Rapids, we were broke. We had to borrow $25 from Cathy's mother to get a new battery. It was thirty below zero and there was two feet of snow on the ground when we got to Cedar Rapids. I was doing the morning show from six o'clock to nine o'clock, then I'd come back to the house, eat a pound of bacon and a dozen eggs, then go back and work from three o'clock to six o'clock. I did two shifts a day and the biggest part of the morning show was announcing who was born. They called it, "What's new in pink and blue?" And my job was to report with great excitement these wonderful life events. Then I'd also have to read the deaths, with great sorrow in my voice. I said, "Man, how did I get into this? And how do I get out?"

That was about the first of January and I got out on the twenty-eighth. But in the midst of that, we'd gone back to Ottumwa for Christmas to Cathy's house. And when we were coming back, it was about midnight, a terrible cold and snow on the ground. Cathy was driving. And all of a sudden, right in front of us from nowhere, was a herd of 150 to 200 horses. There was no way we could stop. I'm thinking, "We're dead. We'll never be able to stop." But all of a sudden the horses parted and we went through. And it was like the horses were never there.

We even went back to look and there were no horses anywhere. We went up to this farmhouse and asked if they had any horses out loose. They said there weren't any horses within miles of there. To this day, I'll never understand it. It must have been another one of these paranormal things that happen to me.

RICHARD HOAGLAND AND THE FACE ON MARS

Somehow I stumbled across a book by a couple of guys who worked at NASA and they had gone through the pictures that were taken on one of our voyages to Mars and the image of a face had appeared in one of the pictures. They'd blown it up and enhanced it and here was this marvelous-looking face. So they wrote a book and they put it out.

The first time I had them on they said, "We're doing this interview from a phone booth because the government doesn't want us to release any of these pictures." And they decided it was probably best not to try to push it.

But I did get a copy of that book and I gave it to Barry Morris from Channel 4 and he said, "Oh, this is wonderful." About that same time a man surfaced named Richard Hoagland who was a former NASA consultant. He was a brilliant, brilliant man and was the science consultant to Walter Cronkite. He had written a book, based on the findings of these other two NASA guys, called *Monuments of Mars: City on the Edge of Forever.* It was a great book, but before I started having him on, it was dead in the water. After I started having him on, the sales took off.

Richard had really gotten into this with all these special enhancements, and what it showed was its face, kind of an ape-like looking creature, with a tear running down its cheek. The message seemed to be, "Here we were evolved, the same as you did, from apes, and we destroyed ourselves. And that tear is our sadness."

I used to ask Hoagland, "What do you think this means?" He used to say, "We have met the Martians and they are us."

Like I always say, the greatest science fiction story is the story of Superman. He had to leave his planet because it was dying and come here to live. So is that what the Martians did, they destroyed their planet – with a nuclear war or something – that forced them to leave their Mars and come here and start the human race? Now, with our intense desire to get back there, could this be our way of "going home again"?

It's a great story. *Monuments of Mars: City on the Edge of Forever.* Here are a couple of reviews of the book:

"I'm fairly convinced that we have discovered life on Mars. There are some incredible photographs [from the Jet Propulsion Laboratory], which to me are pretty convincing proof of the existence of large forms of life on Mars! Have a look at them. I don't see any other interpretation."
- Sir Arthur C. Clarke

"I've seen the studies and I've seen the photographs—and there do appear to be formations of a 'face' and 'pyramids' [on Mars] that do not appear to be of natural or normal existence. It looks like they had to be fashioned by some intelligent beings. For this reason, I have asked NASA to provide assurances that the Mars Observer mission include this [set of targets] as one of its imaging objectives."
- Robert A. Roe, former chairman, Congressional House Committee on Science, Space, and Technology

"I'm sure you're aware of the extremely grave potential for cultural shock and social disorientation contained in this present situation, if the

facts were prematurely and suddenly made public without adequate prepa-
ration and conditioning."

- Heywood Floyd, head, National Council of Astronautics, 2001

WERNER VON BRAUN

One of the smartest men I ever met was Dr. Werner von Braun from Germany. People used to say, "How come the Russians are beating us in the space race?" And the answer was, "Because they have smarter Germans than we do."

I don't know exactly what his connection to the atomic bomb was or any of that, but I knew he was a really brilliant scientist. One day somebody asked him what he knew about UFOs and flying saucers and aliens and all that business. And he says, with no kidding, "You mean you want me to tell you about the snake people?"

What do you think of that?

There was a TV show a long time ago called *V*, that was going to run on Channel 4, and Barry Morse said come on over and preview this, so I did. And the creatures in *V* were venomous snake people who would have fake human heads and when they'd take it off, there was this snake, and they'd eat rats and things.

So that's why they're saying they can't reveal the true identity of these aliens – because they're reptilian and we humans couldn't accept the fact that these beings, who may someday take over our planet, are snakes.

ALI MacGRAW

This is just a quickie about girls who are frisky. This one's about Ali MacGraw. Who would have thought I'd have Steve McQueen's wife on with me? They were married for about five years.

So one day I show up at the studio and they said, "You're gonna have Ali MacGraw on today." I said, "Oh, neat!" I think she was the prettiest girl I ever saw in *Love Story*. There's never been as good a thing as that part she played in that movie.

So she gets into the studio and we hit it off like thieves. During the news, I used to run outside and have a cigarette. So Ali said, "While you're gone, you don't mind if I exercise in here, do you?" I said, "No, not at all! I'll be back in five minutes."

So when I get back into the studio, there she is over in the corner standing on her head. I guess it's some kind of yoga. But the thing was, she was wearing a skirt. And gravity does funny things to skirts when people turn upside down. The question I put to you now is: Was she wearing any panties? Was she or wasn't she? And me, like a dumbass, I had to pick that time to go out for a cigarette break!

MARILYN MAYE

Along with my favorite guest theme, there's Marilyn Maye. And I could write a whole book about my association with Marilyn Maye. One of the great, I mean really great, singers of all time. She is as good as she's ever been, and I used to play her records. I remember the first record I played by her. I was a disc jockey in Indianapolis and I've still got an air check of it. I played, "Step to the Rear" by Marilyn Maye. I thought, "Boy, that woman's really good." And little did I know that she was such a big star here in Kansas City. At the Colony Club on Broadway. So when I got to town, people said to me, "Have you been up to see Marilyn Maye?" And I said, "No, I haven't."

And they said, "Well, you can't go, because she's gone." And she had just closed when I got to town, so I didn't get to see her while she was here. And she'd been at the Colony for ten years, I guess. And she'd gone somewhere. I think she'd moved to Los Angeles, and she was not here.

But Steve Allen had gone to the Colony to see her. Someone had said, "You've got to go see this singer in Kansas City, at the Colony." So Steve Allen came here and heard her and signed her to a contract. And I guess she had a recording deal with Columbia Records, or whatever it was, and they brought her out to Steve Allen's show, and so then she was on the old *Steve Allen Show*, and from there *The Tonight Show* heard about her, and she then set the record for appearances by, I guess at that time, any guest that had ever appeared on *The Tonight Show* with Johnny Carson. Seventy-six times Marilyn Maye was on *The Tonight Show* with Johnny Carson. And whenever she'd sing there, Carson would always say, "You young singers, that's the way you do it."

And so Marilyn and I became thicker than thieves, and I had her on probably more times than any other person as a guest. I just loved her talent. And such a great lady. And just a legend. One time she came to me and said, "You know they're playing my records everywhere all over the country but in my hometown."

And so I said, "By God, I'll play them." And I did. And we became great friends, and are to this day.

I had her do my last studio show at KCMO. She was the last guest I had in the studio and then I had her on my last show at Kelly's. What a great woman. And she told me, too, that Steve Allen said he'd rather be with me than anyone else in the country that had ever interviewed him.

And she would go with Steve Allen and that group to different events and go on the road.

It was Steve Allen and Johnny Carson and Doc, and they'd go on the road to performances. I wish I could have seen one of those.

One of the greatest entertainers this business has ever produced—Miss Marilyn Maye.

SALVATION ARMY SHOW

For years and years and years I did an annual show – the "Salvation Army Show." I started it one year because the Salvation Army had been kicked out of Ward Parkway, or wherever it was. They were told they couldn't solicit and ring their bells. And I felt kind of sorry for them because I always liked the Salvation Army. So I did the show from the parking lot at KMBZ one morning and raised about two or three hundred bucks. And every year after that, I started doing a show to raise some money.

A man came to me one year and he said, "I'd be happy to help you out and raise some more money." And his name was Larry Stewart. After he died, it became known that he was Kansas City's famous Secret Santa, who every year, at Christmastime, would ride around Kansas City in the needier neighborhoods and with his "elves" hand out thousands of dollars to people who looked like they could use it – $20, $50, $100 at a time.

Larry was an amazing human being and he became one of the best friends I ever had. Every year he'd come on the "Salvation Army Show" and he'd sit there with me and Dr. Rich Davis, the father of Masterpiece Barbecue Sauce, another great man, and the three of us would try to raise money for that great cause and eventually we got to the point we were raising over $100,000.

One of the reasons we could do this was that Larry Stewart (Secret Santa) would get up to go to the bathroom and come back in all out of breath and say, "You won't believe this. This guy came up to me and said, 'I was just going through the trash out back and I found this bag with $11,000 in it! I want you guys to have it.'"

So Larry'd bring it in and we'd total it up and let everybody know about our great prize. And before long, other people would start calling in with $3,000, then $5,000, then $8,000. And before you knew it we were up to $92,000 and Larry would say, "You know we're still short of $100,000." He said, "Let me make a phone call." And he'd pretend that he was making a phone call. And he'd get off and say, "I just called a friend of mine and he said he'd give us the $8,000 we need to make it over the $100,000 mark." And what it was, was the Secret Santa coming through for us. Every year big amounts of cash would materialize from dumpsters and suitcases and bathrooms... and it'd all really be coming from the Secret Santa.

Larry was one of the all-time great people in the world. I was so sad when he died last year. He got me out of a jam one time when he was working for Sprint. He'd started a company and he said, "C'mon, let me get you into this." I was broke for about the thirteenth time and he got me into it and made a deal where I made some money.

Larry was like that, always trying to do something nice for somebody. When he got cancer, he went down to the M.D. Anderson Clinic in Houston. He really liked the experience and when he got back he said, "Do you know anybody with cancer?" I told him that I actually did. He said, "Send 'em down to M.D. Anderson and I'll pay their hotel bills." And he did.

Larry Stewart was a true saint, and that's where he probably is right now, up in heaven with all the other saints. Larry Stewart – the Secret Santa.

Larry was always trying to make our Salvation Army show better, so he started flying down the local players from Dyersville, Iowa, who were the ghost players in the great movie, *Field of Dreams*, maybe the greatest baseball movie of all time. I don't know how much that cost him. He'd charter a plane for them, put them up in hotels, buy 'em dinner, and fly them back.

And by then we were doing the show from K.C. Masterpiece Barbecue on the Plaza. So the players would come down in uniform, with a big banner of the cornfield behind them, and we'd get George Brett to come by and sign baseballs. He started coming every year and we'd get George to stand in front of the *Field of Dreams* banner and people could get autographs and have their picture taken with him. We'd also get George to sign baseballs and then auction them off to the highest bidder.

Because I love that movie so much, it was really a thrill for me to have the ghost players from the movie, and the backdrop, and George Brett, one of the all-time greatest hitters here for our annual Salvation Army fundraiser.

JOE ABERNATHY

Joe Abernathy came back to Kansas City to try to put together a deal to bring a station from Liberty, Missouri, to Kansas City to start an FM station. I knew at the time that FM was gonna be the next big thing in radio. AM radio had been kind of sagging in popularity and Joe said, "What this is gonna be is a brand new, 100,000-watt FM powerhouse station at 106.5 on the dial, KFIX. It'll be such a broad signal, it'll take up about one solid inch on the radio dial. And I want you to come and be with me for that."

He said it'd be more money than I was making and at the time I was feuding with my old love/hate nemesis Walt Lothman where I was working. We had these ongoing battles and this one was about a contest we were doing that I thought was rigged. I won't go into details, but I wanted to get away from it because I knew it wasn't good.

So I decided to leave, but my contract forced me to stay off the air for six months. It was a long six months and the night I was supposed to go back on the air they had the Winnetonka High School Band there to play. The station was down in the Plaza, we had crowds ready to celebrate… and we couldn't get the damn station to go on the air. It was a total fiasco.

Well, they finally did get it going and I'd been there for about six months and one day they called me in and said, "This isn't going to work. Here's your pay." And they paid me through the rest of the year

.

RED SKELTON

When I was a kid listening to the radio, because that's what we had before TV, I always thought one of the best entertainers was Red Skelton. And when I was a kid, I always thought his name was skeleton, which I thought was a funny name for a man. How could you be named "Red Skeleton"? I had a picture of these bones and the bones were red. It's funny how your mind works when you're a kid.

Anyway, he had his own radio show and he invented these characters like Clem Kadiddlehopper and Cauliflower McPugg and Willie Lump Lump. They were just hilarious.

He also had a hit TV show and was in a few movies.

So one day he came to town and was scheduled to be on the show and I thought, "Boy, oh, boy, what am I gonna do with Red Skelton?" He was such a big star. So I got with my producer, Rich Meyers, and I said, "Do you have anything from those old Red Skelton radio shows?" And he said, "Let me look," and he found something. And so when Red Skelton walked in the door, we hit the intro to his old radio show that went like this: *"And now, the Red Skelton Hour, brought to you by Johnson's Wax!"*

And he looked up at the speaker and said, "Oh, my God, where did you get that?" It was like he went back in time. And he was such a nice man and we had a great talk. At one point I asked him, "Why did you leave CBS?" and he said, "They told me I was too old." And I thought, boy, that's sad. I said, "How old were you?" I think he was a little over fifty. That's all he was. In those days I guess they didn't want you after you were fifty. Today sometimes it seems like they don't want you after you're thirty-five!

We had a great visit. It was a real honor to talk to such a true American star. Red Skelton, there won't be another one like him.

RUSH LIMBAUGH AND JACK CAFFERTY

I'm gonna tell you some more stories about some people I worked with... Rush Limbaugh comes to mind first because I worked with him in a station in Kansas City called KFIX. I didn't really work with him. I was doing mornings and Rush was doing the evening shows. KFIX was a new FM station in Kansas City.

I remember the day they flew in Larry King for the grand opening. After Larry got here there was some trouble at the station, "technical difficulties," as they like to say. The transmitter, or the tower, or whatever, was on upside down or something, and you couldn't get the station signal anywhere, so Larry King came in to kick off this new station but he never got on the air. I didn't meet him then, but my brother, Pat, did... They had a real good time together, but Larry ended up thinking I was my brother. Larry King's a great guy but he's always called me Pat.

Anyway, Rush Limbaugh was doing nights at KFIX and I was doing mornings and that lasted about six months. So Rush went on to fame and fortune, but before he did, he first went to KMBZ and got fired. Unfortunately, before he got fired, he got my good buddy and fellow DJ, Mother Merz, fired. Mother Merz was a great All-American football player from

Iowa...He was on Rose Bowl teams in the Forrest Evasheski era. So Rush, in a preview of his sweet self, told the station manager that he didn't think Mother Merz was any good. The station believed him and fired Mother Merz. Of course shortly after they also fired Rush. That's radio for you.

One day another guy working in Kansas City named Jack Cafferty called me. I thought Jack was great... He did a show on Channel 4 called *The Noon Edition with Cafferty* or something like that. It was a talk show kind of a thing and I thought he was terrific at it. We hadn't really hung out that much, but one day out of the blue he called me and said, "Could we go have a drink?" I said, "Sure." So I met him at Fitz's Blarney Stone on Broadway. He told me, "You won't believe this, but I just got fired. They told me I was no good. They said, 'You're just no good, get out of the business... Don't ever try to do this again...Be a shoe salesman or work on cars... but don't be in the TV business because you have no talent.' What do you think?" I couldn't believe it. I said, "Jack, you're really good. You've got a ton of talent! You go on and get 'em."

And that he did! He left here and went to Des Moines – I think it was WHO – and became very big in Des Moines. Then they heard him in New York and brought him there, and for thirty years he was the number one afternoon newscaster on NBC...In fact, Dave Letterman used to bring him on his TV show at night because they worked right across the hall from each other. I always thought Jack was great. He's so smart and so good. And now he's on CNN in the afternoon with Wolf Blitzer in that *Situation Room* show. He writes and delivers sensational commentary, just like Edward R. Murrow in the 1950s. I watch him every day. I hope I get to talk to Jack down the road here one of these days and have a visit with him. We'd sure have a lot of stories to trade.

So that's a story about two or three of the guys I worked with who got fired and went on to better things. I continued on in Kansas City for thirty-six years.

QUICKIES

I remember Sid Caesar came along around 1950 with a real popular show called *Your Show of Shows*. I didn't get to see it much because back then in Ottumwa, we were still "watching radio."

But Sid Caesar had some talented people on with him: Carl Reiner, Imogene Coca, and Howard Morris. And they had all these great writers writing for them who later went on to become famous like Mel Brooks, Woody Allen, Neil Simon, and Larry Gelbart.

Imogene Coca came to my show one day and I thought. "Boy, everybody says she's real good," and when she got in the studio she just kind of sat there with me and wouldn't say anything. It was a real nothing, and I'm thinking, "You know sometimes you think something is going to go really well and it just falls flat on its face."

Then there was another one, Red Buttons, and he was one of the people I had on who were Academy Award winners. He got a Best Supporting Oscar for his role as Airman Joe Kelly in *Sayonara*, a great movie that starred Marlon Brando. It was just a short phone interview, but he was really good. He said it was the greatest night of his life when they said, "And the award for Best Supporting Actor goes to Red Buttons."

Red Buttons. He was a great comedian, a great actor, and a great person.

Here's a quick story about Pearl Bailey. Everybody knew who Pearl Bailey was. She was a great lady and a great singer. She also ended up becoming an author, wrote a lot of books. She came to be with me on the show one day and we hit it off... She had a bunch of books she'd written – a couple of autobiographies, a cookbook, and some others. She said, "I want you to take all these books." And she gave them to me and we had a great time and that was that.

Here's a story that still hangs with me. You know, when I was a kid, our whole life in Ottumwa was going to the movies on Saturday afternoons. Every Saturday you went to the movies and you could stay as long as you wanted because they just kept running them. What an experience. It'd start off with five cartoons, then the *Movietone News*, then'd come the weekly serial installment with either Gene Autry or Roy Rogers or Flash Gordon – and his arch enemy, Ming the Merciless – or the Three Stooges. Then you'd get a double feature, a B-movie followed by the current big hit from Hollywood.

Those serials were the original cliffhangers. When I was a little kid I could never figure out how Roy Rogers would get killed at the end of one episode and come back to life in the next!

SHORTS

I'd like to tell some short stories in this book, just some quick takes and one-liner type things. Speaking of one-liners, this one is about Henny Youngman, probably the most famous one-line joke teller in the history of the comedy business.

He's always associated, of course, with his legendary, "Take my wife. Please."

So one day they said, "You're gonna have Henny Youngman on." And I figure, that can't be too bad. He's got all these one-liners, he's performed all over the country for years, he'll have plenty of stories to tell.

So he gets in the studio and sits down and I say, "Hey, Henny, how you doing?"

He says, "Take my wife, please." I say, "Yeah, that's a good one, but how long you been in the business? What'd you like about playing in the Catskills?" He looked at me again and said, "Take my wife, please." And that was about all I got out of him. I tried a third time. "Henny, what're you doing in town?" He said, "Hey, take my wife, please." So I said, "That's all. We gotta go to a commercial."

And that's all I ever got out of Henny Youngman.

After the Henny Youngman disaster, I started finding out that many comedians were often hard to talk to. I thought, maybe I won't have any more comedians on. They seemed to have kind of an evil nature that made them resentful of any interviewer.

But then a guy came to town named David Brenner. I thought he was really funny, in fact he was the heir apparent to Johnny Carson on *The Tonight Show*. When Johnny was on vacation, David would sit in for him and do a terrific job. But somehow, Joan Rivers got involved in it and David wound up getting passed over.

Anyway, I had him on several times. He was just the nicest, most open guy and I really got to like him a lot. He owned a pool hall in Brooklyn and he had almost gotten out of the comedy business. But he told me, "I'm gonna be doing stand up at Stanford & Sons and I'm really worried about attendance." I said, "All kinds of people ought to show up there." He said, "Oh, I don't think so."

Then I asked him, "Why do you think you didn't get the Carson spot?" And he said, "I'll tell you. Once you get over forty in this business, you don't have a chance. They wanted Carson to leave and they wanted somebody younger." And it's pretty much true, when you're over forty in the radio and television business, you're pretty much through. I guess it's that way in a lot of businesses these days.

DAN BOLEN

*I'm Dan Bolen, chairman of the Bank of Prairie Village. I was intro-
duced to Mike Murphy by Ray McGuire, who used to own McGuire Mort-
gage. Ray said that the guy who knew more people and could bring you
more business than a rainstorm was Mike Murphy. Ray organized a lunch
and I met Mike and I think I've been having lunch with him since.*

*At the bank we'd hire Mike to do promotions and advertising for us
and people beat a path to our door. We did a series of ads with Mike in an
interview format and he just has a way of making everybody feel terrific.
The guy comes to life behind a microphone and can make anybody feel
like his best friend. My hat's off to Mike Murphy!*

TALENTED PEOPLE

I never could tell why the people with the most talent, the best looking, the funniest, whatever, why they never thought they were any good. You'd ask them about it. You'd say, "I think you're the greatest thing that ever came down the pike." And they'd say, "Whatta you mean?"

Alice Faye was the most gorgeous woman I ever saw. You older folks might remember her as the wife of Phil Harris from the old *Jack Benny Show*. They were married but they lived in different houses together, right next door to each other. Some folks I know might think that's not a bad idea.

So Alice was on the show one day. She was promoting a line of cosmetics she had on the market. I used to tell any woman with beautiful eyes, "You have Alice Faye eyes." And when I finally saw her in person I said, "My goodness. You are just gorgeous." And she said, "Why would you say that?" I said, "Because you are." She said, "I never thought of myself that way."

Another person like that was the publisher of the *Washington Post*, Katharine Graham.

MALACHI MARTIN

I did a lot of authors on the show. The producer would say, "Here's this book. We're having this guy on tomorrow." Well, I came across one and I said, "Let's do this. A book by a priest. A guy named Malachi Martin."

It turned out he was an assistant to Pope John Paul I, the one who only served for thirty-three days. I asked Father Martin what happened to the pope, and he said he thought the pope was assassinated. There are all kinds of conspiracy theories about this, and many things about the pope's death were mysterious. So I asked Father Martin, "Why was he assassinated?"

He said that the Children of Fatima were told a secret that was never to be revealed, but the pope knew it and was going to reveal what it was. He said, "I was his assistant and I know what that secret was." He said, "Are we on the air?" and I said, "No." He said, "Okay, I'll tell you off the air." I said, "Go ahead, we're not on the air" – of course we were! He said that the secret was – and this was one of the signs of the end of the world – that California would fall into the ocean.

The theory goes that California sits on some kind of geologic cliff and it's a plateau that overhangs the Pacific. There's nothing supporting it. And he said when it goes it's gonna be a certain date -- and that was one of the secrets of Fatima. And the pope said he was going to reveal that and that's why he was killed. I'm sure there are many other theories, but this is the one that Father Malachi Martin told me.

WORLD CONTACT DAY

So Mother Merz and I were working together at KMBZ. He was doing middays ten to two. And we'd cross over in the morning, and he'd come on with me a little bit from nine to ten, and we'd always have fun, and come up with these crazy things to do.

For some reason back then there was a lot of talk about the ASB Bridge and all the pigeons that were crappin' on people's cars as they went through and under and over it.

So I decided Mother Merz and I would go down to the bridge one day dressed in pigeon costumes. So I went out to Kansas City Costume and rented two huge human pigeon suits. With the head and the beak and everything, and feathers all over.

And Mother Merz and I got into these pigeon suits and went down there, and the deal was, we would pay everybody's toll that morning on the bridge. So we did the broadcast down there that morning from six to noon, and we sat there on the bridge dressed as giant pigeons, and for everybody that went across the ASB Bridge – I don't remember what the toll was, a quarter – we paid their toll.

And I thought, "Hey, this is kinda neat. We oughta do this every day. We could do it on the air and everything."

Then there came a day called World Contact Day. I don't know whether it was aligned with Earth Day or what it was, but Karen Carpenter had a song about "Calling Occupants," I think it was, and it was about contacting life in outer space.

It went, "Calling occupants from interplanetary spacecraft." The song made little or no sense, and of course I love things that don't make any sense.

So my idea was to get on top of the Power and Light Building and see if we could bring a UFO or flying saucer in.

So we got balloons printed up, and they said "World Contact Day" on them, and Cathy went to a fabric center and got a bunch of silver satin cloth bolts and she sewed us space suits out of this gorgeous fabric. I still have it – in fact I wore it at for my last show at Kelly's.

We had these gorgeous space suits – silver—and then we got noodle drainers, colanders, and put them on our heads. And I got Hogerty up there with us too. I got him a pair of sunglasses that had windshield wipers on them. And so there were Mother Merz and I and Hogerty up on top of the Power and Light Building with the Winnetonka Band playing out front, on the street below, on Baltimore, and all these people around, looking for what we were doing. Of course, we were doing nothing. We were just standing up there.

And we let these balloons loose, and the band was playing down below, and it was a great day. World Contact Day from atop the Power and Light Building. I don't know how I'd do it again. I don't know how I got up there in the first place. Because I was up that high, and I've got vertigo bad. But there we were.

We did our broadcast from the top of the Power and Light Building, and I always said that the UFO people, the creatures, whatever they are, the snake people, would listen because the signals could go into outer space, nobody knows how far. Who knows, maybe they go from here to eternity, which would be a pretty good title of a movie.

But whenever I would say I was thinking about having a flying saucer show, or whenever I did one – I think it happened about six times – the station would go off the air. It really did. I'd say, "We're gonna talk about flying saucers at eleven." The station would go off the air.

Right in the middle of a show I'd be doing, it would go off the air, and I know six times it happened. Just flat. Signal gone. Can't hear you anymore. Bye-bye. And I always thought they listened to me out there in whatever they're in and they said, "Let's just cut this dude off. Or, we'll signal him to let him know that we're out there."

WALTER CRONKITE

One of the greatest personalities of all time on television was Walter Cronkite. When Walter Cronkite said something on the air, nearly everyone in the country believed him. He was probably the most credible news anchor we'll ever have. He'll always be remembered for the night he had to go on the network news and tell the nation that John F. Kennedy had been killed.

He was born in St. Joseph, Missouri, and lived in Kansas City till he was ten. He started out in radio at WKY in Oklahoma City, but he came to Kansas City to work at KCMO, which is where he met his wife Betsy.

One time I heard he was coming to town and he hadn't been booked on my show. I couldn't find out why he was going to be on some other shows but not mine.

I was climbing the walls to find out what was happening, when about three days before he was due to come, he called my producer and said, "I'm coming to town and I don't know who's handling the bookings, but I will be coming on the Mike Murphy show. That program is my number one priority."

So he came to town and came in the studio and sat down. I said,

"Walter, it's such an honor to have you be here with me." And he looked back at me and said, "No, it's more of an honor for me to be on your show." Wow.

I asked him, "Walter, a lot of people want to know why you quit when you were sixty-five." He said, "They had a law at CBS back then that when you turned sixty-five, you had to retire. They were looking at this kid named Dan Rather so they could get a more youthful presence." Now CBS has done away with that rule. Mike Wallace and Andy Rooney are well into their eighties.

I finally said, "Walter, for one last time, would you do the news for me here on this show?" And he said, "Sure." So we pulled some stuff off the wire and handed it to him. He read it perfectly and it was bringing tears to people's eyes. At the end he said, "And so, for the last time…That's the way it is."

I had told him before, if he'd do it, I'd pay him twenty bucks. When he finished, he looked up at me and said, "Where's the twenty?" So I reached in my pocket and handed it to him and he put it right into his pocket. Then he said, "I want to sign an autograph here for you." My producer came in and gave him this $150 pen that I'd given the producer for Christmas. He signed the autograph and put the pen in his pocket, too. And away he went. There'll never be another one like him. And that's the way it is.

GERRY SPENCE

Gerry Spence, famous for his buckskin jacket and flowing silver hair, is one of the most renowned trial lawyers in the United States and has had more multimillion-dollar verdicts without an intervening loss than any other lawyer in America.

He defended Imelda Marcos. (Remember her? She had two million pairs of shoes or something.) But Gerry was a terrific guest and he and I got to be real good friends.

One day he came into the show with the best looking woman I ever saw. And she was his "driver." She was gorgeous, about six-foot two and built like a brick outhouse.

I said, "Hi Gerry, who is this?" And he said, "She's my driver." I said, "Do you like her?" He said, "Hell, do I like her? I love her!"

Gerry was really a funny, good guy. He came on the show all the time and one day he said, "You know what?" I said, "What?" He said, "I have a lot of friends, but you are my best friend." I thought, "Whoa, that's pretty extreme! Why would Gerry Spence say that I was his best friend?" But it was a great compliment.

KELLY'S

One of my favorite places in Kansas City has always been Kelly's Westport Inn. It's supposed to be the oldest building in Kansas City, at least they've got a plaque on the wall that says it is.

In 1950 an Irishman from County Clare named Randal Kelly turned it into the famous place it is today. One night after St. Patrick's Day, Randal came out to our house and looked at me and said, "Mr. Murphy, this is the finest house I've ever been in!" It really wasn't that great, but it was nice of Randal to say that.

I was at Kelly's for the fiftieth anniversary in 2000 and we hung a time capsule from the ceiling. I've got a lot of memories about Kelly's... after St. Patrick's Days, after the parades.

But one Halloween, the story had come out that Kelly's basement was haunted. Nobody'd been down there much and with a building that old, you figure there's gotta be something going on. There were rumors they used to trade slaves down there. Take 'em down and manacle them. Some of them would die down there.

So I asked if I could go down there and do a show on Halloween and see if we could resurrect some kind of a ghost or spirit or something. They said, "Sure, go ahead."

So before I went down there I wanted a psychic with me, her name was Pat Brown. I called her and said, "I'm doing a Halloween show from the basement of Kelly's and I want to resurrect some ghosts. Can you do that?" She said, "Yes I can, but how do you get to Kelly's?"

I thought that was pretty funny. I said, "Well, if you're a good psychic, you oughtta know." And even after I gave her directions, she wound up getting lost.

Anyway, we got there and I had Art Brisbane with me, who was a great writer and worked at *The Star* for many years. He came to write about what we did.

Pat the psychic finally showed and went into a trance alongside these stalls where they supposedly kept the slaves. It's Halloween Eve. I asked her, "What do you see?"

She doesn't say anything. Total silence. I said, "This is radio. We've gotta do something."

Well, it went on and finally she said, "Yeah, I think I see something. But I'm not sure."

I'm thinking, "What? That's it? What kind of psychic is this?" You'd think at least she could've made something up! But that was my experience with psychics.

LEN DAWSON

One of the greatest guys I've ever met is a man named Len Dawson. He was one of the first guys I met when I got to town. He said, "I'm gonna take you to lunch." And we went to the Playboy Club. We had a great visit and when the bill came, he said, "Now, I'm gonna pay for this."

He opened his wallet and he had eight or nine hundred bucks in his wallet, and that was in 1969 or so and that was a lot of money. It still is. I said, "Lenny, why do you have all that money in your wallet?" He said, "When I was a kid I never had any money, so when I got some money I said I was always gonna feel like I had some, so I always carry eight or nine hundred bucks." He probably doesn't do it today in the era of credit cards. But I thought, "Boy, that's neat. What a neat guy."

So Lenny and I became really good friends and when his wife, Jackie, had her stroke, Len would do her hair and get her all fixed up every day. Lenny took great care of her. Here is this great all-star quarterback of the Chiefs, who'd won the Super Bowl, and he's taking gentle care of the woman he loves. What a picture.

He said one day, "Jackie likes fish." I said, "Well, let's go to Romanelli's and we'll have the catfish." And we did. So every week or two Lenny and I and Cathy and Jackie would go to Romanelli's for the catfish. We did that for about a year and Jackie got better, but whenever I'd see Lenny, he'd say, "Let's go have a catfish." And so we did that for a long time.

Those were great days in this city, after the Chiefs won Super Bowl IV, beating the Vikings 23-7. Their great stars would be seen everywhere: Lenny, Jim Lynch, Willie Lanier, Bobby Bell, Ed Budde, Jan Stenerud. They were like gods.

Whenever we wanted to have one of the Chiefs do an appearance, I'd call Ed Lothimer, a former Chief and proprietor of the famous End Zone restaurant. I'd say, "Ed? I'm standing behind your house and I want to take you to a deal we're doing." Ed said, "Whattaya mean you're standing behind my house?" I'd say, "I'm sending a helicopter to pick you up." And we had Officer Link fly the helicopter and go land in Ed's backyard, pick him up, and take him to wherever we were going.

Ed always thought that was the funniest thing. Ed'd call me up and say, "Hey Murph! Go stand in your backyard. A plane's gonna pick you up." Those old Super Bowl Chiefs were always ready to help out and have some fun and they did all these things for nothing.

To show you how times (or maybe, people) change, when Marcus Allen was with the Chiefs more recently, he had a book out and we called and asked if he'd like to come on the show and talk about it. They said, "Mr. Allen would be happy to come on your show. The fee will be ten thousand dollars. Thank you very much."

.

BIRDHOUSE TO THE RESCUE

I have a lot of January stories. The one I want to tell happens on January 12. Cathy was pregnant with Susan. I was working in Moline and we were living out in the country in Orion, about thirteen miles from town.

Cathy said it was time to go to the hospital. So I called my buddy Birdhouse, who lived near us, and I said, "Birdhouse, I don't have any gas in my car and Cathy's got to go to the hospital to have Susan. Can you come out with some gas?" So he brought out a couple of gallons to put in our car and I'll never forget it because it was *twenty-seven degrees below zero!* That's not wind chill, that's actual temperature. And we got to the hospital and Susan was born the next day at Moline Public Hospital. And if it hadn't been for my buddy Birdhouse bringing the gas, Susie would've been born in the woods. So thanks again to my buddy, Birdhouse.

THE LAST SHOW

I gave notice I was going to leave about six months before and they called it "The Mike Murphy Sunset Tour." We'd do the show from different locations. We'd always call them "the last show," and then we started a countdown. First there were thirty shows, then there were twenty, then there were ten, and so on.

When it got time to do the last show, they said, "Where do you want to do it?" I said, "Well, I think it's gotta be Kelly's." We went to Randal and Kyle Kelly and set the date for December 14, 2004.

We called it "The Final Deception." I didn't really mean to call it that. At one point I called it "The Final Defecation," and I thought, "Wait a minute, that's not right!" So it stayed "The Final Deception."

And for the third and last time, I wore my space suit with the alien head and everything. And I didn't think anybody would show up. I just figured, here we're doing this final show and who would care enough to get out of work and come? I guess everybody fears that. You know, you have a going away party and no one comes?

Anyway, I get there about half an hour before the show's supposed to start at nine o'clock, and just like I feared, nobody was there. Then all of a sudden people started to show up. I'm sitting there at the bar at Kelly's wearing my old space suit. The people keep coming in and saying hi and by the time we had to go on the air, the place was pretty well filled.

I looked at the sign on the door and I think it said "Capacity: 780" or something. So once the show got going the place really got packed and I thought they'd lock the door and not let anybody else in.

Well, my great friend and former mayor, Charlie Wheeler, got there and couldn't get through the crowd to be on with me. But eventually all the mayors came: Charlie Wheeler, Kay Barnes, Dick Berkley… Emmanuel Cleaver, former mayor, now congressman, came in and walked up to our broadcast desk and knelt down and said, "Oh, Noble Thing and Leader of the Cat People, would you give me your blessing?"

I thought that was really neat. Emmanuel Cleaver was one of the most charismatic guys I ever met. What an honor.

Then we had the music people: Bruce Bureman and Eddie Delahunt and Nathan Granner, the great tenor who performed at so many of my shows. And last but not least, The Elders with Ian Byrne from County Wicklow, Ireland. What a great group. They sang and played Irish songs, and everybody was just in shock they're so good. There were a lot of tears in a lot of eyes.

All the talent that was there, it reminded me of the old *Ed Sullivan Show*. And the only regret I have is that I wished I'd talked to the people more. I hope they all know how much I love them.

It was a great way to end a show and a great way to end a career. The last show at Kelly's.

THAT'S ALL FOR NOW

I'm doing the final chapter of this book from Kelly's (Kelly's Westport Inn, to be precise). It seems very fitting to be doing it here because this is also the scene of my last radio show, almost four years ago.

We're doing it right alongside of the shrine they made for me on the day of the last show. To have a shrine erected to you is really something.

There's a big neon sign at the top that says, "The Final Deception. 12/17/04." My portrait is on the wall under it, in a beautiful frame. I'm holding a stein of beer and I've got my Kelly's shirt on. It's pretty damn good. It was painted by a guy named Bob Carson, a great artist.

It's so neat to come into a place like this, a world-class place like Kelly's, and have your picture and a neon sign above your head. And I'm surrounded by other great characters Thomas Hart Benton, Buck O'Neil, Tom Pendergast… some of the greatest characters that ever existed in this town are on the walls of Kelly's. Believe me, it's quite an honor to be among them.

The Hallowed Halls of Kelly's. I did my show one time from Kelly's basement, which I think was supposed to be haunted. And I've been friends of all the Kelly family over the years. There's so much Kansas City history here and so much of my own history, it seems fitting to have done my last show on 12/17/04 here and now the last chapter of this book, sitting here with my old pal, Steve Jackson, who's been responsible for putting this all together.

It's a rainy day and it's time now to say: Good Night, I Love You and Goodbye.

AFTERWORD

By Steve Jackson

Writing this book with Mike Murphy has been one of the supreme highlights and absolute joys of my life.

Mike and I met quite by accident in one of those magical acts they call kismet or serendipity or plain old Irish luck. I met him during a recording session he was doing. He said he needed a ride home and I said, "I'm going that way." (Which actually was a lie. I just wanted to get Mike Murphy in my car so I could meet him and talk with him, this famous "Voice of Kansas City.")

It was a great ride. We found we shared many common interests and world views, we liked to laugh and trade stories, and I think we both had a love of the world and its people. When I dropped him off, he invited me to join him and his cohorts at an informal weekly lunch they had at a local pub. I assured him I would. And I did.

That was about three years ago and we've rarely missed a week. I'd been a writer all my life, and at one point I suggested I help him write a book about all his amazing stories and adventures. He said he'd think about it.

From time to time I mentioned to Mike the possibilities. I thought the people of Kansas City would love to have a book of his most amazing stories, interviews, and shenanigans. I offered to do all the "heavy lifting," transcribing, editing, spell-checking, etc. All Mike had to do was to dictate these marvelous stories while I recorded them. Finally, he agreed and the seeds for this unique collection were sown.

After nine months and over fifty thousand words, over one hundred stories, it seems like we were just getting started. So you never know. If you see Mike and me some afternoon, sitting in the Salty Iguana or Kelly's or the Corner Cocktails or O'Neill's, we just may be working on Mike Murphy, Book Two. Just follow the laughter.